HAUNTED BELFAST

HAUNTED
BELFAST

JOE BAKER

First published 2007

Reprinted 2008, 2009, 2011

The History Press Ireland
119 Lower Baggot Street
Dublin 2
Ireland

www.thehistorypress.ie

© Joe Baker, 2007

The right of Joe Baker to be identified as the Author
of this work has been asserted in accordance with the
Copyrights, Designs and Patents Act 1988.

All rights reserved. No part of this book may be reprinted or reproduced
or utilised in any form or by any electronic, mechanical or other means,
now known or hereafter invented, including photocopying and recording,
or in any information storage or retrieval system, without the permission in
writing from the Publishers.

British Library Cataloguing in Publication Data.
A catalogue record for this book is available from the British Library.

ISBN 978 1 84588 589 2

Printed in Great Britain

Contents

Introduction	7
Cavehill	9
Ghostly Warnings	13
Lucifer's Match	18
The Ghost of the Belfast Workhouse	20
The Schoolhouse Haunting	26
The York Street Police Barracks	29
The Belfast Synagogue	32
Ghosts in the Waterworks	36
The Ghosts of Sailortown	39
The Ghost of the Duncairn Estate	42
The Suicidal Ghost	44
Behind Bars	46
The Strange Haunting of John Street	49
The Disturbing Ghost of Glengyle	51
The Ghosts of the Lord Kelvin	55
The Ghost of the University	59
The Infamous Galloper Thompson	63
Jubbie the Tram Chaser	67
A Sandy Row Ghost Story	69
The Ghost of Ballymacarrett	72
The Victoria Barracks	75
'Scottie Shoe' – the Ghost of the Grand Central Hotel	80
The Pipe Lane Mill Haunting	84
A Tragic Belfast Haunting	87
Ghostly Nun at Ballynafeigh	93

Introduction

What you are about to read in the following pages is a collection of ghost stories from all over the city of Belfast. I have no doubt that there will be many readers who will dismiss them outright as nonsense but this is not a reflection on the authenticity of this publication but rather a result of the skepticism that often surrounds the topic. I, for one, remain 'sitting on the fence' because I have never seen a ghost so I cannot say for certain that they exist, but then again I have never seen the wind either yet I know that it is there.

Ghost stories are always fascinating and even more so when they are about our own city. Most of the stories I have included are from the Victorian era when such tales were rife.

Over the years I have collected hundreds of ghost stories from all over Belfast. When I come across a story the first thing I do is check it out, and by this I certainly don't mean staying overnight in a creepy old house. As the following pages will show, most ghost stories are based on a tragedy so I usually check historical records to see if such a tragedy actually occurred. If it did not then the story is false and can be completely dismissed. For those not based on a tragic event I would generally check to see if the individuals and places concerned existed.

The following events really did occur and the people connected with them did exist. The only section which I can't confirm is the sightings – no one can!

Cavehill

Today when we think of the Cavehill we think of the zoo, Belfast Castle and its surrounding area of natural beauty, the caves or McArt's fort at the hill's summit. However, almost 100 years ago many people were visiting the area, not to see any of the above attractions, but in the hope of seeing a ghost which was said to be roaming the hillside.

In 1913 many people who had visited the Cavehill at night reported hearing a wailing noise coming from within the woods. They had stated that it sounded like a man crying and that he was in a great deal of distress. Some of those who heard the sound investigated and ventured into the darkness of the trees to search for the unfortunate man. Those who did so found that the noises got louder until they appeared to be nearing the man, at which point they would disappear.

The matter was reported to the police a number of times. They searched the area twice but with no success. At various dates from then on the police were still receiving reports of the noises but were now dismissing the whole episode as the workings of a practical joker. However, two years later the reports changed dramatically.

In June 1915 a man and woman were out for a walk in the area. As they were approaching the castle they noticed something ahead of them which appeared to be floating within the trees. The man decided to take a closer look and, leaving the woman standing by the pathway, walked in among the trees. A few moments later he came stumbling down the hillside and, after grabbing the girl, ran from the area.

After calming down and knowing that he was within the safety of the Antrim Road area, he told the woman what happened. He stated that when he got closer he saw what appeared to be a man who was hovering in the trees. He watched for a few seconds and when the figure moved slowly towards him, he ran back towards the path, falling a number of times. He later had to be treated for cuts and severe bruising. News of the sighting spread and dozens of people flocked to the Cavehill, hoping to catch a glimpse of the apparition, but all went home disappointed. The police soon got to hear about it and decided to stick with the theory that it was a practical joker who had now gone too far. They investigated and some of those who 'knocked about' the area were even arrested, but once again there was no definite answer.

The story soon died away and was not heard again until five years later. In September 1920 two teenagers approached the caretaker of the castle and told him that they had seen someone in the trees and, as it was dark, they were too scared to go down the path alone. The caretaker, believing it to be poachers, agreed to see the pair down and the trio set off towards the Antrim Road.

Cavehill.

When they got to the point where the youths saw the man the caretaker had a closer look with his lamp but discovered nothing, not even a sign of a poacher. He then told the teenagers that there were ghosts reported in the area some years ago and that he and his fellow workers had had trouble due to the amount of people coming to the area hoping to catch a glimpse of the mystery apparition. The teenagers laughed at the story and set off home towards the Antrim Road. After seeing them out of the grounds the caretaker then set off back to the castle. When he got to the area where the boys told him of their sighting he saw a man standing, looking into the trees. Still thinking that he was a poacher, the caretaker shouted a warning to him but the man completely ignored him and moved into the trees. The caretaker dashed towards him and, shining his lamp, found to his horror that the man was floating about two feet above the ground. Dropping his lamp he ran to the castle and told a workmate what he had just seen. The two men remained within the castle until the next day.

Once again numerous sightings were reported after this but the most significant was in March 1922. A man out walking his dog was strolling along the path when he noticed another man just ahead of him. When he passed, he noticed that the man was staring into the trees and had not moved, remaining in the one spot. The observer noticed that his dog was crouching down alongside him, growling slightly. He continued and allowed his dog off the leash. On his return down (which was approximately an hour later) he was surprised to discover that the man had not moved and was still standing and staring into the trees. With his dog off its leash he noticed that the animal would not go near the other man. The walker then approached the man to see if he was alright but to his shock he disappeared before his eyes. He ran home and told his family of what he had experienced.

A few weeks later two men, John McAleavey of Alexandra Park Avenue and Frederick Orr of Duncairn Gardens, were walking in the area when they approached what they believed to have

Cavehill.

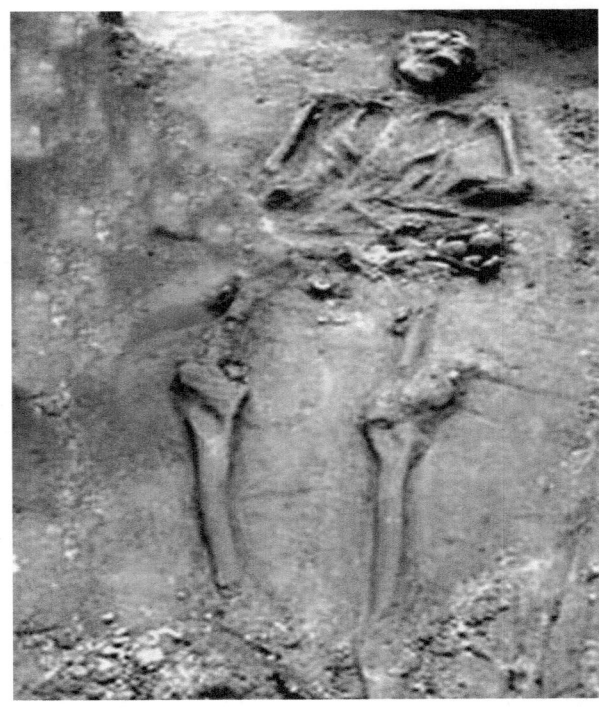
Skeletal remains.

been an unusual looking rock. To their horror they found it was actually a human skull.

The men immediately reported the findings to the police at Chichester Road who sealed off the area where they recovered a full skeleton. Some bits of clothing and an old pair of boots were attached to the bones, while alongside them were found a small empty medicine bottle and a teacup. A weather-eaten penknife and part of a watch chain were the only articles found in the clothing. All was removed by a Sergeant Greeney and two constables. The police appealed for information and published a description of the findings in the local press. When they did so a woman came to the barracks and identified the belongings as those of her husband who had disappeared some time ago. She said that his name was John Scott, originally from Waringstown, and had started his own business as a tailor. It was stated that all parties concerned believed the man had taken his own life.

The site in which the skeleton was discovered was the area in which all the previous sightings occurred and the police were mystified as to how they had never discovered it before. One theory for this was that it may have been covered in bramble. After the remains were buried the ghostly sightings were never seen, or heard of, again.

Ghostly Warnings

Often when apparitions appear there is a reason. One of the most common reasons for a haunting would be the appearance as a form of 'supernatural warning' to the living. In fact, one of the world's most famous ghost stories is centred on such a warning and concerns the Irish Lord Dufferin.

The ex-Viceroy of India looked death in the face, but he didn't recognise it – not then. All that Lord Dufferin knew was a sudden cold, repellent feeling, a feeling of shock, which made him step backwards from the window of the great country house. His Lordship was not a man to be scared. Soldier and diplomat, he had travelled the world, unflinching under fire, cool and self-possessed in vital affairs of state. He had joined a house party at the home of an old friend in County Wexford, relaxing after his years in India with a few pleasant days of fishing and shooting in the Irish countryside. Close on midnight, after the port and brandy had gone round and the gentlemen had finished their cigars, Lord Dufferin made his way to his bedroom in a comfortable frame of mind. It was a spacious room and the log fire in the wide hearth spread a feeling of warmth and well-being. Lord Dufferin was at peace with the world and prepared for bed. He read a few pages from a novel, and then settled down to sleep.

But sleep would not come. He dozed and kept waking, twisting and turning. It was unusual because, calm-minded man that he was, he normally slept easily and deeply. As he lay there, that night in 1890, something very like fear took hold of Lord Dufferin. It was a sensation he was not used to, and it disturbed him so much that at last he got up. He walked slowly to the window and drew back the heavy velvet curtains. The moon was full in a cloudless sky and a brilliant white light flooded the gardens which stretched away beneath his bedroom window. He could see every rise and fall of the sweeping, cropped lawns; clumps of shrubs threw back shadows. Nothing moved. But Lord Dufferin, deep in contemplation of the beautiful scene, felt impelled to stay gazing intently from his window.

Suddenly, a movement in the shadows riveted Dufferin's attention. He watched, fascinated, as into the moonlight a figure stepped. It was a man, walking slowly across the wide lawn, and carrying what looked like a large box on his back. Bent almost double, the man walked to the centre of the lawn. Then he stopped, lifted his head and looked straight at Lord Dufferin. In the moonlight the watcher from the window could see the man's face quite clearly and the sight of it made the ex-Viceroy take an involuntary step backwards. It was a face, he said later, 'of horror and malevolence' that made him shudder as their eyes met.

The man then turned and walked away into the darkness of the shrubbery, but not before Lord Dufferin had become convinced of the burden the figure carried—a coffin.

The Lord Dufferin.

It was now nearly two o'clock in the morning and the big house was silent. Lord Dufferin waited for a while at the window, but everything was still again. He pulled the curtains, went back to bed, trying desperately with his logical, disciplined mind to explain this startling sight. He was too matter-of-fact to believe in ghosts—he had seen enough mysterious happenings in India and believed stolidly that there was a down-to-earth explanation for everything—but there was no way he could explain this night's experience. He insisted later that what he saw was a real, solid, living man; there was nothing ghostly about him, just an eeriness which had given him that cold feeling of revulsion. Oddly enough, Lord Dufferin afterwards recalled, the feeling disappeared almost immediately, and he slept soundly.

At breakfast the next morning, Lord Dufferin mentioned what he had seen from the window. The man-with-the-box story raised a few eyebrows and a laugh or two, but no one took it very seriously. His host insisted that there was no history of a ghost around the place. The episode was therefore dismissed as a nightmare. So that was that.

Afterwards Lord Dufferin often visited his friend in Wexford, stayed in the same room even, but he never had that feeling of chilled dread and certainly never saw anything odd. So far as he was concerned, it was all over—or so he thought.

After a number of diplomatic appointments, Lord Dufferin was appointed British Ambassador to France. One morning he was due to speak at an important meeting of diplomats in a Paris hotel. The meeting was on the fifth floor and when the Ambassador arrived, he was escorted to the lift. The lift doors opened and Lord Dufferin, deep in conversation with a secretary, allowed

The Royal Hospital.

a number of people to go in first. The he stepped forward. As he did so, the uniformed lift-attendant faced him. The years rolled away in a flash. Lord Dufferin stared in amazement and then stepped backwards out of the lift—just as he recoiled from that bedroom window in a silent house in Ireland five years earlier. For the face of the lift-attendant, the eyes that held his for a brief moment, they were the face and eyes of the man he had seen in the moonlight, the man carrying a coffin across the lawns of a quiet country garden.

Once again he felt that chill dread soak into him. So shaken was he that, to the astonishment of the hotel manager, he waved the lift away. The doors closed. The lift whined upwards towards the fifth floor, leaving the Ambassador standing with his secretary. As he waited, speechless and agitated, Lord Dufferin heard a sudden harsh clanging and banging, followed by a terrific crash which vibrated through the hotel. Immediately there was pandemonium. Hotel staff rushed around madly, calling for doctors and ambulances. Their panic brought the Ambassador back to normality. He hurried to the foyer and there an agitated hotel manager poured out the awful story. The lift had just reached the second floor, where, in a few minutes, Lord Dufferin should have been addressing the assembled diplomats. But the lift doors never opened. With a scream of tortured metal, the wire suspension cable snapped. The loaded lift plunged down the shaft, carrying shrieking helpless passengers, and smashed into the hotel basement. Five people died. Among them was the lift operator, the man whose face had stopped Lord Dufferin from stepping into the cage. The strangeness of it did not end there. Dufferin learned that the lift attendant had been engaged only for that day, replacing the regular attendant who was ill. And no one ever discovered his proper name, or where he came from.

Tomb Street.

The story has become part of the Dufferin family history, and the present Lord Dufferin says of the incident: 'It is perfectly true, but my grandfather could never explain it. We have always believed the story and puzzled about it, because he did not believe in ghosts.' And the man was real—his body in the hotel basement proved it.

As stated previously, this is the most famous case of a 'supernatural warning'. However, there are many others and the city of Belfast is the host to at least several. Of all Belfast's ghost stories, the one most definitely categorised as being a 'supernatural warning' would be the incident which occurred in Tomb Street at the turn of the last century.

Number 2 Tomb Street was the Waverly Hotel. Although it was named a 'hotel' this establishment was more similar to a lodging house. At this time it was owned by a gentleman named James Spence and because of the close proximity to the Belfast docks the Waverly did a 'good turn' with all the foreign visitors and seamen. In November, 1903, nineteen-year-old Sarah O'Hare was employed as a housemaid in the Waverly. Her job was to awake every morning at five o'clock and prepare the common room for the guests. She was then to tidy their bedrooms and make the beds when the guests were at breakfast. At around midday she was permitted to return to bed for a few hours, to her sleeping quarters in the building's attic. In the evenings Sarah's role was to help the kitchen staff tidy up and, when finished, her duties for the day were complete.

One night in March 1904, when Sarah had finished her kitchen duties, she decided to go out for a walk. At around ten o'clock she returned and retired to bed. In her room she lit the oil lamp and prepared for bed. She lay under the blankets in order to heat up and after a few moments she reached out to turn off the lamp. When she was about to flick it out the bright figure of a girl suddenly appeared out of nowhere and stood alongside her bed. Startled, Sarah jumped back and as she did so the figure disappeared before her eyes.

Terror gripped young Sarah and she ran screaming from the room. Some of the guests went up to the room and, after discovering nothing there, they went down to the common room to see what had happened. After the girl settled down she told her story.

Two of the guests then went back up to her room to check it, and after seeing that everything was alright, one of them went over to turn off the lamp. As he was doing so he hesitated and called over the other guest. After examining the lamp both of them returned downstairs. They then told the girl that had she turned off the lamp, it would have exploded.

Was the girl saved by the appearance of a ghost in her room? It would seem so. At this time accidents connected with such lamps were occurring on a regular basis. The most common cause was a type of cheap oil which was being used and, because of its low price, it was commonly used among the poorer classes. Approximately forty people were killed per year as a result of these accidents, and hundreds injured. So why should Sarah O'Hare have received a warning, when seemingly no one else had? The answer to this question will never be known, but the only reasonable explanation is related to an incident which occurred some years earlier.

On the night of Tuesday 30 April 1895 Jane Wilson was at her home at 43 Tomb Street. Just after midnight her mother called her up to go to bed. As she extinguished the lamp it exploded, turning the girl into a ball of flame. At the same time Harbour Constable McHenry was walking along Tomb Street when he saw a flash and heard screams coming from the house. When he burst in, Jane's mother had put blankets around her, but these were also on fire. The constable pulled off the blankets and was able to put out the fire. Jane was rushed to the Royal Hospital in Frederick Street but she died a short time later. Jane Wilson's death was the sixth in Belfast that week as a result of lamp explosions.

As stated, Jane died in Tomb Street and, in general, ghosts would appear to be territorial. Did the ghost of Jane Wilson warn Sarah O'Hare of her impending death?

Lucifer's Match

Another Smithfield story is centred around a dreadful fire which occurred in 1882 in the Lucifer Match Factory in Millfield Place. The factory was owned by a Mr Samuel Osbourne and was managed by Mr Samuel Johnston. Many of those who worked here refused to call the works by its proper name, as they thought it extremely unlucky, and choose instead to call it 'Osbourne's Match Factory.'

On Friday 15 December 1882 a lad named Mullan was working in the drying area when he accidentally stood on something which caused a small spark. The spark itself landed in among the drying racks and almost immediately the whole room was engulfed in flames. The workers rushed out shouting 'fire, fire' to alert the rest of the staff. At the upper section of the drying room there was a smaller room which was used by those who were employed to box all the matches and inside were two boys and two girls doing just that. The only entrance to this room was through the main room which was now totally ablaze. The four were trapped and they all began to scream for help with one of girls screaming out for her daddy. All the workers outside could clearly hear the screaming and the girl crying for her daddy was, in fact, the daughter of the factory manager, who was also outside.

He immediately began a number of rescue attempts and on one occasion he was pulled back as he went to run straight through the flames, receiving severe burns to his face and hands. At this point the fire brigade arrived and a few hours later the fire would be put out, but everyone knew it was too late for the four trapped. The badly burned bodies were found, removed and identified as being:

John Brown, aged 17, 23 English Street.
John Phillips, aged 18, 7 Quadrant Street.
Mary Lavelle, aged 16, 23 Cupar Street.
Maggie Johnston, aged 16, 14 Wilson Street.

After the fire an inquest was held in nearby Divis Street and its findings were that the victims 'came to their deaths through suffocation and the effect of burns; and further, the jury do recommend that the said match factory be conducted with greater care and caution in the future.'

A short time later a new factory was built and work once again commenced. The word 'Lucifer' was dropped from the factory name. A year later residents living around the place were

A young match girl.

awakened by screams which appeared to have been coming from the factory. The matter was reported to the police and the gates opened, with two constables making an inspection. Nothing unusual was found and the place was locked up.

The following day the workers began to talk about the previous night's incident and they connected these screams to the fire. The following night nothing else was heard and the whole area remained quiet for around another two months. This occasion was very much the same as the first with everyone being awakened but one of those who heard it claimed that she heard the words 'daddy, daddy' through the screams and that she knew it was the same scream as the young girl who died. A number of others agreed and stated that they heard the same thing.

The following day the story began to be told throughout Belfast and that night a large crowd assembled around the match factory to listen out for any strange screaming, but to their disappointment nothing was heard. The screaming sounds were reported for a few years afterwards until the factory was demolished in the early part of the present century. When the factory disappeared, the screaming sounds disappeared with it.

The Ghost of the Belfast Workhouse

Throughout the world there are many ghost stories connected with warnings. Ireland, and indeed Belfast, is no different. There are many tales of supernatural warnings throughout the city and a few of them are recorded in this publication. Without doubt the most famous of all Irish ghosts is the banshee. This is a particular haunting where the apparition of an old woman or beautiful girl warns of an imminent death within one of the ancient Irish clans. Today there are many people who claim to hear the wailing of the banshee, but this is more likely to be a cat in heat. Not because a banshee does not exist but because the clans they haunted do not. As stated, the banshee is not alone in the supernatural world for giving warnings – there are many, many others. One case is said to have occurred in Belfast during the last century and, although the apparition did not appear previous to every death, it did when the death was suspicious. This was the ghost of the Belfast Workhouse.

In the early 1800s the British government introduced a new system to Ireland – the Poor Law. Before this the government believed that the poor were to be punished as beggars and many unfortunate people with no source of income received cruel 'solutions' such as flogging and transportation. Part of this new system was to be the construction of new institutions which were to be simply known as 'workhouses.' A number were built throughout the country and Belfast was one of the towns to obtain one. This was built on a site next to the road which led to Lisburn. In these houses the punishment for being poor continued and paupers had to live through very harsh conditions and no matter what state they were in, they received no sympathy from the people placed within these establishments. Because of this, the poor only went to the workhouse when they were on the brink of starvation. If a family were forced to go they were instantly separated, forced to do useless manual labour and made to sleep in horrendous conditions. Food was given in very small portions and at times it was just about enough to keep them alive. As mentioned above, those who were placed in charge of the workhouses were very cruel and unscrupulous towards fellow human beings and, although always denied, often inflicted injuries through their numerous assaults. Sometimes these assaults led to death and when this occurred numerous details were deliberately kept back at inquests so that a jury would find death due to natural causes – a verdict which was often reached without the jury even seeing the body.

Throughout the 1890s and the early part of the last century, numerous stories were told in Belfast about a ghost said to haunt the workhouse. It is unknown just who the ghost was supposed to have been but it was said only to have appeared whenever certain individuals died within the complex. After being seen a number of times it was learned that this apparition only appeared when a death within the house occurred in suspicious circumstances.

It is unknown just how far back the story goes but one of the early sightings occurred in 1894. On Thursday 26 April of that year one of the workhouse paupers died in the lunatic section of the buildings. John McKeown was placed in this department after he struck a man while working in nearby fields. The housemaster in charge that day was the despised Hamilton Douglas and it was he who ordered McKeown to be placed in the lunatic section, even though he was of sound mind. Douglas kept the pauper locked up night and day and eventually McKeown slowly became insane. In the records his death was recorded as 'exhaustion' which is an interesting conclusion for a man who was never allowed out and was chained down in a cell. Facts were hidden from the inquest jury and when they inquired as to why his body was covered in bruises they were informed that these were caused by 'numerous falls.' Once again, all this from a man chained down. Those confined within the workhouse knew what happened to McKeown and who was responsible. They also knew that he was not insane, but all were powerless to speak out about it in case they received the same treatment from Douglas.

On this occasion the inquest jury were not completely fooled and had their suspicions. With no proof they made recommendations that the rules concerning the confinement of paupers in the lunatic section should be changed. What the outcome should have been was for Douglas to face very serious criminal charges, but this was a time when the poor were barely regarded as human beings.

The night McKeown died all the other paupers were in their cramped sleeping quarters at the usual time of 8.30 p.m. and, because of strict rules concerning quietness, the whole building was in total silence. Later the same evening a commotion was heard in the 'master quarters' which were situated above the main entrance. It remains unknown exactly what the disturbance was but a clergy man connected to the institution later recorded in personal notes that a 'strange figure was seen in ragged clothes and that it had disappeared without leaving the room.' The following day stories began to circulate that John McKeown was back to seek his revenge on Hamilton Douglas. Many of the poor within the institution obtained great delight in believing this story but soon there were no more sightings and the story and the case of McKeown were forgotten.

In September the same year another sighting was reported and again was recorded in the minister's personal notes. On this occasion it was claimed that a similar apparition appeared in the women's dormitory of the main building. Shortly after 'lights out' one of the inmates ran from her bed screaming. She ran to the main door and after finding that it had been bolted she became hysterical. Needless to say the whole dormitory had been awakened at this stage with most of the girls too terrified to approach her, not from fear of her, but because of the workhouse rules. The night porter arrived and soon after the girl was taken to the infirmary. After being calmed down the girl said that she had seen a ghost. It had been looking out of one of the windows and then disappeared before her eyes. She remained motionless for a few seconds and then ran. She remained in the hospital wing until the following day and then left the workhouse.

At the same time as the sighting another incident was taking place in the workhouse - in the lunatic ward. An inmate named Alexander Donaldson had died. On 13 August Mr Donaldson was placed in the hospital due to a mental illness and two days later removed to the lunatic ward. Like McKeown, Donaldson was also chained down and again was treated in a brutal and wicked way. His death occurred at the exact time the apparition was seen in another section of the buildings. Again, like McKeown, his cause of death was suspicious but as usual the inquest, which was held in the workhouse boardroom, was forced to find a more reasonable explanation.

Belfast City Hospital was built on the site of the old Workhouse.

This time the death was recorded as 'congestion.' There is no doubt, judging from the original inquest report, that the unfortunate man suffered from a mental disorder and was prone to occasional fits but in the harsh environment of the Belfast Workhouse there was no pity or help and he was simply thrown into the lunatic section and chained down. His was not the only case where this occurred but today we would suspect that most, if not all, were cases of epilepsy instead of mental conditions. Mr Donaldson's death was forgotten as the sighting of a ghost in one of the wards caused more excitement. Soon afterwards, when news spread of the circumstances of Donaldson's death, inmates began to conclude that the sightings only occurred after a death. Not just any death, as these were occurring almost every day, but suspicious deaths – those that may have been murder.

The inmates were not the only ones talking of these strange deaths in the Belfast Workhouse and the fact that they always seemed to be taking place in the lunatic ward. The Poor Law Guardians also noticed that something was not quite right and they demanded a report. Once again another cover up was compiled but a small section of it makes interesting reading:

....With regard to the condition of the insane in the workhouse, the inspectors state that they are compiled to reiterate the opinion that it is far from satisfactory, and they think that where the lunatic inmates of these wards manifest symptoms that render them obnoxious to others, or whether they are so helpless as to require individual care, the lunatic wards of the workhouse as at present constituted do not provide suitable accommodation for them.

Through this report it was being admitted that paupers who were insane should not be placed in the lunatic department. However it mentions nothing about how these people were treated by the people who were supposed to be looking after them. It also 'brushed over' the circumstances of McKeown who was not insane at all but who was locked in there by Douglas.

Another sighting was reported on 11 November 1894 and this time it was in the lunatic section itself. This part of the institution consisted of two wards located at each side of the infirmary building. It was a two-storey building and the wards had no windows. At the entrance was situated the 'master's' office and next to this were the stairs which led to the upper floor. On the above date a porter (who was usually an inmate of the institution) saw the figure of a man standing near the stairs. The area was in darkness and when he looked out of the 'master's' room the man, who was in ragged clothes, was standing in front of him. Thinking that it was an inmate the porter came out of the room to see what was going on. The man had completely gone. There was no way that this man could have got out other than going up the stairs and if he had done this, the porter would have seen him. No one went near the stairs. The porter was scared and went to the 'master's' quarters and reported what had just happened. They had not heard of the previous sightings and quickly connected the incident to an occurrence on that spot a few days previous. A man named John Nelson left the hospital and, once outside, fell. When discovered, he was carried back inside but died on the stairs. The porter and 'master' thought that this was a ghost of that man but unknown to them another incident was being 'taken care off' at the same time as the sighting. It was in the lunatic ward.

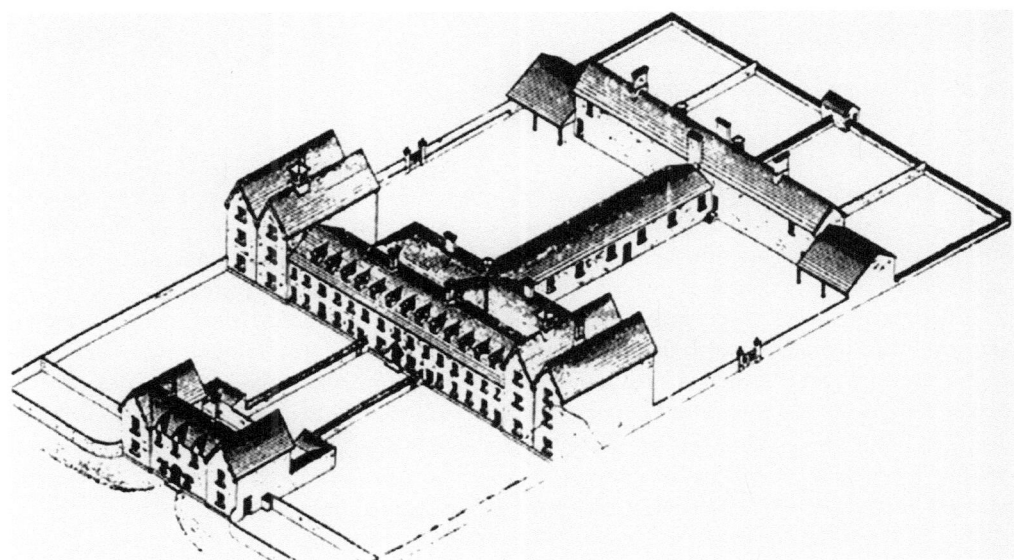

A sketch of the Belfast Workhouse.

An artist's impression of inhabitants of the Belfast Workhouse.

Thomas Stewart died and an inquest was held on the 13 November, again in the workhouse boardroom. In the traditional cover up it was recorded that Stewart died from 'exhaustion' but the jury went one step further. They added that they 'were recommending their (lunatics) removal to a properly equipped asylum where they would be properly treated.'

'Where they would be properly treated' – why had the jury added this to their report if Stewart's cause of death was 'exhaustion'? It was now obvious that this apparition was only appearing every time someone died suspiciously and the story was now being told all over Belfast. What was happening to these unfortunate people was that they were being branded insane by a non-medical 'master' and placed in the lunatic department when, occasionally, it was nothing more than an epileptic fit. Because they had no control over their actions these people were also being cruelly mistreated, as they were being chained to the floor.

One of the next sightings, and one of the strangest, connected with this series of events occurred not in the workhouse but a few miles away from it. On Thursday 2 May 1895 Sarah McCreevy was sitting in the kitchen of her home at 10 Portland Street in the York Street area.

At around 10.00 p.m. she decided to go to bed and after extinguishing the gas lanterns she lifted a candle and holder and made her way upstairs.

When she reached the top of the stairs there in front of her was the clear figure of a man dressed in ragged clothes. She stared at it for a few moments before running away, screaming. She ran to a neighbour (Mrs Isles) where she described what had happened. After hearing the screams a few other neighbours came to see what was going on and a few of the men went into the house to investigate. Nothing and no one was found. On describing the details, Mrs McCreevy said that the figure was floating as she could see the floor below it. She spent the rest of the night with Mrs Isles.

The following day an official from the workhouse came looking for Mrs McCreevy. Neighbours informed him that she was not there but was staying at another house. After finding her the man informed her that her husband, who was a workhouse inmate, had died in that institution the previous night. He had been confined in the lunatic ward.

The institution continued in operation up until the Second World War. When it closed down it was converted into a hospital and although today a few of the original buildings remain, the modern tower block of the Belfast City Hospital occupies most of the site of what was once the Belfast Workhouse.

The Schoolhouse Haunting

It is a well-established fact that the vast majority of ghost stories are in some way connected to a tragic event and that the victim of that event is generally stated to be the apparition. Throughout the whole of Ireland there are very few cases where more than one apparition has appeared at the same time and of these few cases there are at least four within Belfast. One example occoured when two apparitions were sighted in the old Smithfield Mill after a number of people were killed when a section of the building collapsed. In this case a ghost was sighted by a number of people in one of the working rooms while another was seen to disappear in the stairway. Another Belfast story, which not only features a number of apparitions but also a number of different paranormal events, is centred around one of the most tragic events ever to occur in old Belfast. This series of events was known in Victorian Belfast as 'The Ghosts of Raglan Street.'

Raglan Street was a typical turn of the century thoroughfare which connected Cyprus Street to Albert Street in the lower Falls area. Within this street stood St Peter's National School which was the main school in the area for a number of years. In December 1894 a performance came to the school and it was decided to hold it in one of the upstairs classrooms, which was larger than all the others in the building. Many children from the surrounding streets attended the show and some of them were accompanied by their parents.

When the show began a few of the boys in the front rows began to misbehave and because of this, those in the seats behind were forced to stand on their chairs in order to see the performance. As the show was progressing all the gas lanterns suddenly went out and there was a loud shout of 'ghost!' The whole room was in total darkness and widespread panic broke out, with the children shouting and crying. A rush was made for the door and when it was opened it was discovered that the hallway was also in total darkness. Those who were first out the doors were pushed out into the hallway by the crowd behind them. They could not see where they were going so many of them fell down the stairs while others stumbled down over them. Those who fell the whole way down the stairs were blocking the door which led onto the street and in a few moments they had the full weight of all those who were on the stairs on top of them. This not only made the situation worse for those unfortunate enough to have fallen, but all the children on the stairs now began to scream in terror. Peter Cassidy, of 55 Cyprus Street, was one of the few parents who had attended the show. He had taken his four year old daughter to watch the performance. After the incident he made the following statement:

The entertainment commenced about a quarter past five o'clock. There was a brave lot of children, and a good many women in the room. The front part was packed thick enough, but there was some vacant space at the back. I should say that there were between 200 and 300 there. The performance had started about half an hour when the gas went out. There was a good deal of confusion before this. The boss of the show came out first dressed up and began singing 'Come, all you little children.' The children were shouting, however, and the man could not get leave to sing, and he had to stop. He went into the classroom behind and brought out his wife to help him, but they would not listen to her either, and she went in, too, and sent out the little girl. They would not hear any more than the others, and kept shouting and kicking up a terrible noise, but I heard little of their singing or speaking. Then the light, which had been very dim all the time, went out, and left us all in black darkness. There was a rush by the people behind for the door, and then the children in front got terrified, and scrambled over everything, trying to get to the door too. I was towards the front, and I picked up my little girl and put her in the little room behind out of the rush, and went the length of the stairs to try if I could find a light any how. There must have been a horrible crush on the stairs at that time, though I could not see. The women and poor children were shrieking and screaming. The children ran over each other and tumbled to get to the door and some of the glass in the windows was smashed. When the gas was lighted I did my best to help free the children as soon as I had taken care of my own little girl. I can't say who put out the gas, but it was a fool that did it anyhow. It caused a heap of trouble, not to speak of loss of life.

John Dickson, of 39 Tenth Street, was returning from his work at Dunville's Distillery when he heard the screams coming from the building. He later stated:

I was about the first in, and at considerable risk held the door forced partly back, while I got out one or two of the children. At first we could not open the door for the crush, and afterwards the pressure was so great as to threaten to close it again. I was coming home from work when I heard the shouts and shrieks for help inside. When I got right inside at last, the gas was soon afterwards lit, and I saw a sight on the stairs that I'll never forget. The poor children were lying just like bags of meal, one on top of the other, and in some cases tied into each other as it were. We at once got to work as quickly as possible, taking them out into the air. There was a crowd round the door by this time. One little fellow I took to the house opposite the school, but the poor chap died on my knee almost directly afterwards. He was the last I took out, and he was right at the bottom of the heap at the foot of the stairs. I took a little girl home who seemed very bad, but she got better after a time. I would say there were over fifty children on the stairs.

After everyone trapped in the school house was calmed down, those who were injured were removed to nearby houses with the more seriously injured conveyed to hospital. As this was going on it was discovered that four children, Eddie McKeown, John Connell, Dennis Dwyer and Rose Taggart, had been crushed to death. A police investigation was immediately launched and as statements were being taken from all those who were in the building one of them, a man named Neil O'Donnell, stated that he had heard a boy named John McManus tell another boy named John McKenna to 'turn off the gas for a geg,' a few minutes before the lights went out. The police arrested both boys and held them in custody pending further inquiries. Both youths were held in cells adjourning the Belfast Police Courts and, according to the old R.I.C. records, one of them was extremely restless and was 'making up stories.'

John McKenna on his later release claimed that as he was held in his cell he could not get any sleep due to a number of disturbances. He claimed that whenever he tried to get some sleep a

An upstairs classroom.

mysterious tapping sound would keep him awake. After some time he called on the attendant to find out what the noise was but when this man entered the cell the noise had stopped, but no sooner had he left the room when it began again. This noise continued the entire time McKenna was held, a noise which no one else heard, and as a result, he got very little sleep. After the Coroner's inquest the following week, both boys were released as no one had actually seen them turn off the gas. However, unknown to them their troubles were only just beginning.

On his release McManus left Belfast and went to stay with relatives in Co. Tyrone. When McKenna returned home he could not leave his house due to the ill feeling towards him throughout the neighbourhood. This feeling was to escalate when a number of unusual episodes occurred at the school house, episodes which terrified all the children who attended the school.

One of the first incidents occurred over the Christmas holidays. Sounds were heard by the locals of classrooms being destroyed and windows being broken. The police were called but when they entered the building everything was found to be in order. This same incident was reported a number of times but the police believed that it was someone playing a trick on the residents. These were not the only incidents however, as there were others which terrified the children during schools hours. The gas lights glowed abnormally bright on several occasions but whenever they were checked by corporation gas inspectors, they were all found to be in perfect working order. When no explanation was found, some parents kept their children away from the school with others being transferred elsewhere. A number of rumours also circulated the area suggesting that a few of the children were struck by objects which were thrown at them from seemingly nowhere. There is no evidence of this happening and it is believed that these were 'dramatic additions' to the original stories.

John McKenna heard of these stories and connected them to the sounds he heard when in police custody. Terrified, and facing community hostility, McKenna decided to leave Belfast. In January 1895, he moved to Co. Kildare where he was believed to have joined a religious order. After he left, there were no more reported incidents in the schoolhouse. Neither McKenna nor McManus ever returned to Belfast.

THE YORK STREET POLICE BARRACKS

Like any other city Belfast has a massive amount of invented ghost stories. Some, such as the so-called Trinity Street ghost, have gone on to become well known and, by some people, believed. Most simply die away and are forgotten. These fabricated stories are made up for a number of reasons and commonly involve work places in which people stay alone overnight.

When Belfast became a city in 1888 a number of new R.I.C. barracks were opened up in various parts of the city and new recruits were usually the first victims of these 'ghost stories.' Quite often the main story centred on a dead sergeant or inspector who had committed suicide inside the building. These stories continued to be invented well into the present century. They were generally dismissed but there are two known, confirmed cases which are connected to police barracks in Belfast.

One concerns poltergeist activity in the Glenravel Street barracks. Other than quite basic details, nothing much is known about it other than the fact that it centred on the deaths of a number of constables killed in the base during the Luftwaffe blitz of 1941. The other concerns a number of sightings which took place in the old York Street barracks.

This was situated at 94 York Street a few doors down from the junction of Little Georges Street. It was a large three-storey building and before it was taken over by the police it was used as a temperance hotel. After the First World War the building was taken over by a man named John Monteith and was shortly renamed 'Monteith's Temperance Hotel.' A few months afterwards, members of Mr Monteith's staff began to tell of various strange sightings. It was claimed that the ghost of an elderly gentleman was observed strolling around the ground floor, makings his way from the back corridors to other sections of the building before turning a corner and disappearing. One member of staff who saw it stated that the area where it vanished was closed off and led only to a small social room with no other way out. The stories continued but were dismissed by Mr Monteith as false until he himself saw it. Mr Monteith not only witnessed the ghostly figure but also recognised it as that of the previous owner, Ben Herring.

In 1927 the police took over the building and the sightings continued, with basically the same story. Ten years later a strange incident occurred in the building which was almost certainly connected with the apparition of Ben Herring. A drunken man was arrested in nearby Ellins Court for a domestic dispute and placed in a cell to sober up. A few hours later the man was heard throughout the barrack screaming and banging on his door.

A number of officers went to see what the problem was but after they opened the door the prisoner, in a wild state of panic, pushed past them, ran down the corridor pushing others out of the way, and escaped.

HAUNTED BELFAST

York Street Barracks.

York Street map.

Much to his wife's annoyance, the man returned home breathless and exhausted. He then told her a strange story of what happened to him in the barracks. A few hours later the story began to circulate the area—a prisoner waking up in his cell with a man standing over him, suddenly disappearing. The prisoner, frightened at what had just occurred, then began to bang on his cell door to get out. Later he returned to the barrack and was charged with escaping from police custody and told to appear in court a few weeks later.

When in court, the man's sighting was described in great detail and it was argued that he fled the cell more in terror than a deliberate attempt to escape. The police were then asked about this sighting and the sergeant in charge told the court that there had indeed been other sightings on previous occasions. The court asked if any were recorded in the station book and were told no.

The man then received a small fine and was not imprisoned, as was the norm in such a case. No doubt the story had an influence on the judge's decision.

The Belfast Synagogue

Many of Belfast's older generation will remember a time when the main Jewish Community within the city was based in the lower Antrim Road. These Jewish citizens were based mainly within the district between the Antrim Road and Cliftonpark Avenue and the community began to grow in earnest after Belfast became a city in 1888. At this time the city's Jews were worshipping at their synagogue, which was in Great Victoria Street, but at the turn of the present century it was decided to create a new synagogue in the heart of the Jewish population. A suitable site was discovered in Annesley Street off Carlisle Circus and soon after building work commenced. When completed the new synagogue was perfect and everything seemed fine, that is until some of the local members began to hear stories of a terrible tragedy which occurred on the site some years previous.

Elizabeth Fitzgerald was an elderly woman who had lived on the opposite side of Annesley Street. She had been a very private woman and most of her day was spent looking out her front window at the open field facing her. During the latter part of the 1870s she had been watching children play in this field and because of the noise they were making she went out and told them to play at the opposite side of the field. The children obliged and went towards some new houses which were being constructed facing onto the Crumlin Road. These houses backed on to the field and the children began to play on the wooden frames which were around them. A short time afterwards a loud crash was heard and a large cloud of dust went up around the area where the children were. Some of those who lived in Annesley Street rushed over to see what had happened, and when the dust settled it was discovered that one of the frames had collapsed with a large pile of bricks on it, killing two of the children instantly and badly injuring some of the others. The small district was devastated and none more so than the old woman, who was now blaming herself for what had happened. The woman died a few months afterwards and the sense of guilt which she carried upon herself was taken to the grave.

In later years the stories in relation to this tragedy were not centred on the fatal event but focused instead on rumours that ghostly apparitions of the old woman had been seen in different parts of the street. The house in which Elizabeth Fitzgerald lived had been No. 9 and the family who moved into it after her death had told their new neighbours of strange incidents within it, ranging from actual sightings of the old woman through to the behaviour of their youngest child who was terrified to go into the front downstairs room. The family stayed here for a few years and after they had moved elsewhere the house was then taken by a Mr James Webb. After he had settled in the neighbours had informed him of the experiences of the previous family and although Mr Webb had not actually seen anything, he later told that there was sometimes a 'bad atmosphere' in parts of the house.

On one occasion Mr Webb had been returning from work and after getting off a tram on the Crumlin Road he walked down Fleetwood Street towards his home. As he was doing so he looked over at his house and noticed that the curtains hanging in the front room had moved. He rushed into his house but saw that nothing was amiss and that all the windows and doors had been closed tight. Later when talking to his neighbours about it he added that the strange atmosphere had been present.

During the construction of the new synagogue one of the workmen involved had fallen from the roof as he was placing a roof beam across. He was taken to the nearby Mater Hospital where he received treatment for his injuries and where it was discovered that he had received a broken arm and leg. The following day he received a visit from two of his colleagues and during the conversation he stated that he had seen an old woman in the site and asked what she was doing there. His friends were mystified and told him that they had seen no one but that they would ask when they returned to the building. When they did return no one else had said that they had seen the woman and when a few of the residents approached to inquire how the workman was, they were asked if the woman had been anyone who lived in the streets or those behind it. It was then that they were told the story concerning the old woman who once lived in No. 9. Predictably most dismissed it as superstitious nonsense but others had a different view due to the sincerity with which the story was told to them. There were no other events to add to the story, so, as could be expected, it soon died away and nothing more was heard about it until the outbreak of the Second World War.

A section of Annsley Street after the Blitz.

Annesley Street Synagogue.

In April 1941 the German Airforce carried out a massive bombing raid on Belfast. Many areas of the city were devastated and many people were killed. Annesley Street was no exception and most of the houses in and around it were totally destroyed, including No. 9. When the bombers had gone and the 'all clear' given, some of those returning to what was previously their homes said that they had seen an old woman in among the rubble and that when they went to offer assistance she had disappeared. Many had put this down to a 'trick of the mind' after what they had just been through, but some of the older residents who remembered the original story had told others that it must have been the ghost of the old woman who was said to have haunted the street thirty years previously.

In 1937 the Adler family living in Mannheim had been seized by the Nazis and put into a concentration camp in Lublin, Poland. The family's daughter had survived this as she had been staying elsewhere and soon afterwards she became one of a number of Jewish refugees who arrived in Belfast from Germany. On her arrival twenty-six-year old Sadie Adler was fortunate enough to obtain employment in a city centre radio store and lodgings in Fairview Street in the Crumlin Road area. In 1942 the American Army arrived in Northern Ireland and many of the younger girls in the city began to date them, Sadie Adler being one of them. On Saturday 12 September, the pair had attended a Jewish New Year's service in the synagogue. Both of them had noticed an old woman who had been standing near the wall at the far side of the room. They had found this strange as she was not taking part in the service, and she was being ignored by all those near her. When the couple looked again she had gone. After the service the pair were talking to some friends and mentioned what they had seen. No one else seemed to have seen her and the soldier thought this impossible, as the woman would have had to walk past some of them to leave and she could not have done this without being observed. The couple then went to the home of some friends who lived in Kinnaird Street. During their conversation they mentioned the old woman in the synagogue and how they thought it strange that she managed to leave the building so quickly without disturbing the service. As they were describing what the old lady looked like, the elderly father of their friends told them that there had been sightings of an old woman in this area before and that she was supposed to have been a 'banshee-type ghost' who warned of some pending misfortune. Later the same evening the friends decided to part company and the American went with Miss Adler to see that she got home safely, as there was still a blackout in operation. They left with another couple and when they crossed Annesley Street they were talking and laughing about the story which their friend's father had told them. A few moments later both were struck by a passing bus. The American was killed instantly and the girl was badly injured. She was rushed to the Mater Hospital and was said, on her arrival, to have told one of the nurses about the old woman sighted earlier. She died a few hours later.

This is the last known story connected with the sighting of the old woman. As previously stated, much of Annesley Street was totally destroyed during the German bombing raid, with only two of the houses remaining. After the war the street was redeveloped and a factory was built on the site of the bombed houses.

During the 1960s the synagogue itself closed down and the building was taken over by the Mater Hospital but now lies derelict. The street was again developed in 1993 and the factory was cleared to build a new nurses' home.

Ghosts in the Waterworks

There are several ghost stories connected with the Antrim Road Waterworks. Over the years many people have reported diverse sightings, ranging from gentlemen dressed in period clothing through to people splashing about in the water. One of the most interesting concerns the sightings of a tall well-dressed man who has been seen in the upper section of the grounds strolling and suddenly disappearing. There have been many different theories as to who this may be but the most likely seems to be that it could be the ghost of John Herdman.

On May 15 1862, John Herdman was at home entertaining some friends. At about 5.45 p.m. he apparently left in the company of Mrs Eleanor Thompson to take a stroll through the waterworks in North Belfast which was a place of resort even back then. They walked from the house, down the avenue through the grounds and out towards the road. When they reached this junction they turned right in order to enter the waterworks by the entrance gate and since Mr Herdman was a resident of Cliftonville, he had his own personal key to the entrance gate to use at his leisure. On this day however, it was later revealed, previous arrangements to walk up to the Cavehill were postponed in favour of a stroll through the waterworks' grounds. As they passed along the road they engaged in quiet conversation. It was a clear evening and we can understand the peace and tranquillity that might have existed there, for it was from this picturesque quietness that the area derived the name 'Solitude'.

While they were walking along they noticed a man coming from the direction of Mr Lyons' estate. That man was Mr William Herdman, John Herdman's cousin and a man very much known to him. As he got nearer he asked John for a moment of his time in order to discuss some private matter. John apparently tried to dismiss him and while both he and Mrs Thompson walked on, a shot rang out. In terror they both turned to see William Herdman, his hand outstretched, taking deliberate aim. They both tried to flee towards the Lyons' gate but instead they both fell. Mrs Thompson had tripped over her dress but John Herdman had been shot and critically injured. As they both tried in vain to rise and escape from the gunman, another shot rang out. John Herdman was reported to have cried out, 'Oh God, I am killed, call for my wife'.

Perhaps the ghostly figure which has been haunting the area around the waterworks for many years is indeed a lost soul, so to speak. Perhaps it is the ghost of this poor murdered man still trying to deliver a message to his wife, or attempting to reveal further secrets of the tragic affair. Several days later a public funeral proceeded from Mr Herdman's home at Cliftonville. The solemn procession was watched by thousands of the city's residents as it led its way across the city to the little graveyard by the church at Newtownbreda where the family burial plot was situated.

The Waterworks.

The Antrim Road Waterworks.

His cousin, William Herdman, was brought to trial that same July. It transpired that he was supposed to receive money from his aging aunt. This money was to have been a type of allowance and its handling and distribution was left in the capable hands of a Mr Russell who acted as Miss Herdman's agent.

Owing to his drinking and gambling however he believed that his cousin was advising his aunt to hold back some of that money. This was untrue but the matter ended in the tragic death of John and the imprisonment of his cousin.

The strange and eerie happenings in and around the waterworks area are not a new phenomena. Behind Solitude is the archaeological site of an ancient Irish fort, or 'rath' as they were properly known. The site is just above the bridge which some time ago played host to a steam engine track. This miniature train used to carry children around the area beside the plots at the upper pond and many entertaining hours have been spent there from time to time. The ancient fort which is situated in the vicinity was at one time regarded with great respect. What were later described as mere superstitious beliefs by the so-called learned and literate classes who later populated Belfast were nevertheless religiously revered by the majority of people who lived in the locality. These beliefs and customs had been handed down through every generation in Ireland and predate Christianity. Bad luck was said to befall anyone who interfered with such a holy site as it held beneath its surface the cavernous palaces of the supernatural *daoine sidhe* or 'fairy folk'.

Today this reverence for our rivers and earth is becoming more and more fashionable. One only has to look at the popularity of herbal remedies and alternative medicines against the manmade drugs which everyone has grown so used to. No wonder then that the waterworks with its rivers, ponds, underground streams and ancient forts, should be the host for supernatural occurrences from the earliest of times to the present.

The Ghosts of Sailortown

As the name of this area would suggest, Sailortown was a large section of Belfast's dockland community which stood on the County Antrim side of the Belfast Lough. The area itself is now long gone with interlinking roads and railways replacing this once proud and historic community. There were hundreds of old ghost stories set in this area and many of them are being told right up to the present day. There were tales of an individual family being targeted by a very violent poltergeist while others told of a certain spot in the area where a young child was shot dead during the disturbances of the 1920s.

On this occasion nothing was actually ever seen, but many people stated that they felt themselves being pushed onto the roadway when they walked past this spot. This occurred a number of times to a large number of people and after a while those passing would step onto the roadway themselves.

Another tale centres on an incident that occurred sometime during the 1930s. One of the many dockside watchmen was visited every night by the captain of a foreign ship and, even though there was a language barrier, the captain could speak a bit of English and they would have a chat. One particular night however the captain did not show up and, thinking that he must be working, the watchman thought nothing of it. The following night was the same and, as the watchman wanted to see the captain before the ship went in a few days time, he approached one of the ship's crew. The man he went to could speak no English but found another who could. The watchman explained that he usually had a chat with their captain and mentioned that he had not been feeling well over the last two nights, asking if the captain was now feeling better.

The crew member looked at him in total disbelief and asked the watchman to describe their captain. The sailor then told the watchman that their captain had committed suicide by hanging himself as they came into Belfast, and that his body had been placed in another ship going to their country—two days ago.

Another of the stories from this area is about the ghost of a woman killed in Steam Mill Lane, which was on the fringes of the Sailortown area. Steam Mill Lane was a narrow street facing the old headquarters of the Harbour Police. In February 1928 two carts were coming towards each other on this lane and when they met, one half mounted the pavement to allow the other past. The cart on the footpath was carrying large paper rolls which were being delivered from a warehouse to a nearby newspaper office. As it dismounted the footpath, the sudden jerk caused one of the rolls to fall off, landing on top of an unfortunate woman who was passing at the time. The woman, who was well known in the area, was killed outright and was buried a few days later.

Left: *Sailortown*.

Below: *An aerial view of Sailortown*.

Steam Mill Lane.

A few days after the incident a man was sitting at his door in nearby Bradford Square when he saw the woman walk right past him towards Steam Mill Lane. He then rushed in to get his wife but by then she had completely disappeared. They looked up and down the lane but there was no sign of her anywhere. The man then went down to the woman's family home, which was at the corner of Steam Mill Lane and Gamble Street, to inform the family of what he had seen. The dead woman's youngest girl answered the door and the man asked if her older brother was in (the father had been dead for a number of years). When the son came to the door the man informed him of what he had just seen and added that he understands it to be strange but that he knew what he saw. The son paused for a few moments before looking up Steam Mill Lane. He began to cry. The man apologised for causing the distress but reiterated that he had definitely seen the boy's mother, to which the boy replied that it was alright, because he believed him. Apparently, it had been the fourth such sighting since his mother was killed.

The Ghost of the Duncairn Estate

Today it would be hard to imagine the New Lodge area in North Belfast as a part of the open countryside, but just over one hundred years ago that is exactly what it was. At this time a large section of the area was taken up by the Duncairn Estate and within this stood two large mansion houses known as 'Duncairn' and 'Duncairn House'. These were occupied throughout their history by numerous wealthy Belfast citizens. The name Duncairn is an Irish word and its basic meaning is 'monumental pile of stones.' Before being named Duncairn House this mansion was known as 'Fortfield' and it is from these names that we can assume that an ancient fort or monument stood within this area. This estate occupied the large area between North Queen Street and Haliday's Road on the right hand side of the New Lodge Road. Within it stood large open gardens (which gave the name to Duncairn Gardens) and it was within these that the ghostly sightings were reported.

During the 1870s those who occupied both mansion houses decided to re-landscape the whole grounds. A team of gardeners were employed to undertake this task and soon after work began. The gardeners laid out new flower beds, planted new shrubs and laid out a maze. As they were doing this work one of them reported seeing an elderly woman sitting nearby. The man pointed her out to the others and they all later admitted seeing her. One man went over to see if she was all right and as he was doing so she disappeared in front of him. The gardener was totally stunned and immediately ran back to the others to tell them what happened.

They then set out to enquire about the woman and approached the house. They went to the servants' quarters to ask about the old lady and were told that what they had seen was the ghost of Widow McNulty. The servants then added that she had been seen on a number of previous occasions and always by people new to the estate. Ten years later the estate was being demolished to clear the way for a new housing programme. As the houses were being dismantled a number of the workmen stated that they had seen an old woman walking around the overgrown grounds. One of them said that he had seen her going into one of the mansions and after searching it found no trace of her. He added that there was no way she could have left the building without being seen. A short time later the entire estate was cleared and the streets which occupy the site today were constructed. Since then no further sightings were reported of the Duncairn ghost known as 'Widow Mc Nulty.'

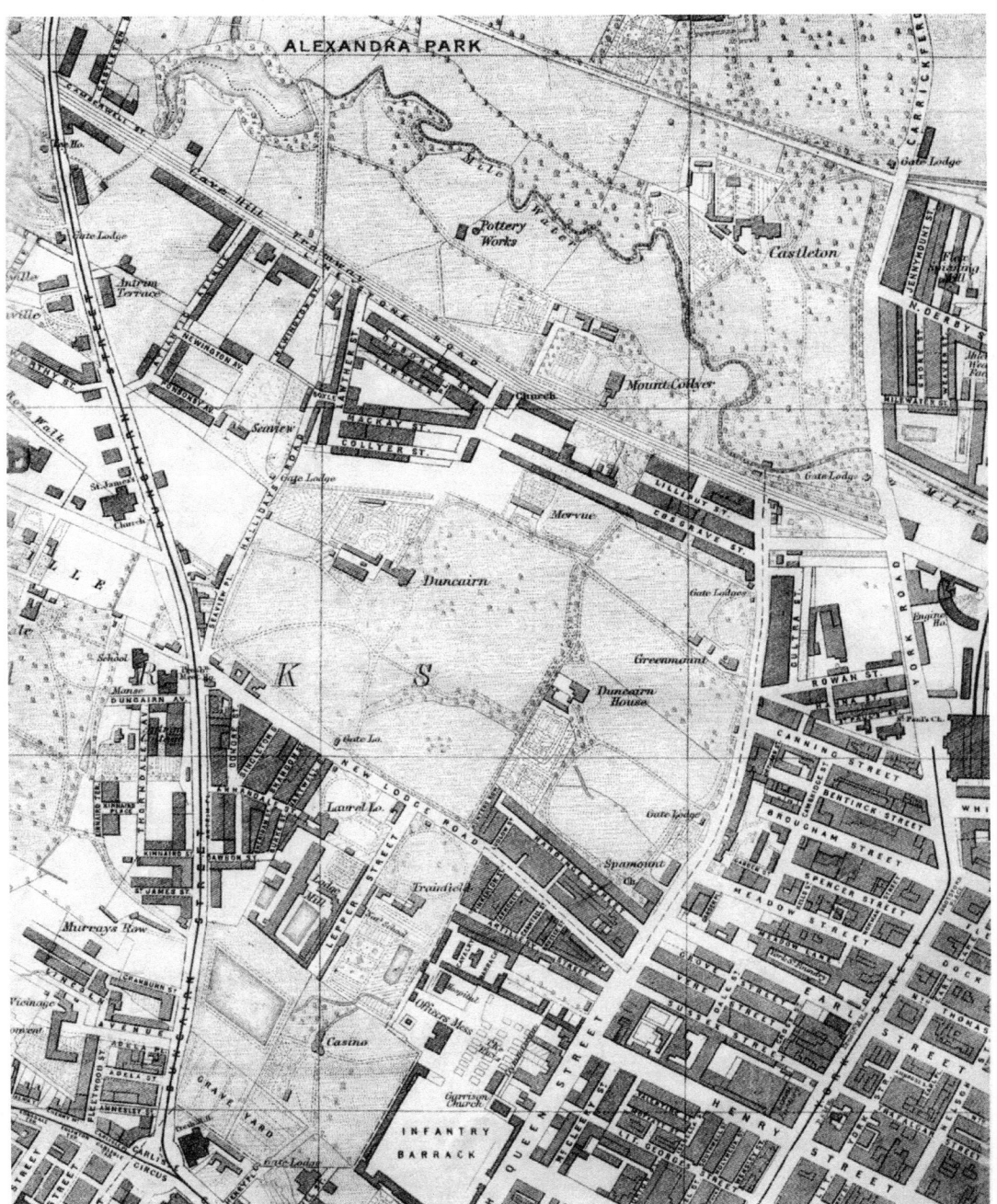

Duncairn Estate 1888.

The Suicidal Ghost

Many years ago various stories were told of a cloaked man, who it was stated was seen by many people, standing on the Queen's Bridge. There would appear to be nothing strange about the above statement, but it was added that whenever people turned away, even for a split second, the figure completely disappeared. There were many different theories on this ghost and who it had been, but the most common was that it was an unknown person who had committed suicide by jumping into the dark waters below.

The story began around 1910 when a man, who was passing over the bridge on his way to the shipyard, observed a strange looking man wearing a large cloak standing on the opposite footpath. He turned to his friend but when they both looked, the man had gone. The shipyard worker then looked up and down the bridge but there was no sign of the person he had just seen. Thinking that he must have jumped over the bridge, he ran to the edge and looked into the water but again there was no sign of anyone. He ran to a constable and told him that he believed that someone had just jumped into the water. The police man went over to the spot where he saw the man and, after looking over, told the man that this was one of a number of recent sightings all of which stated exactly the same thing. Knowing that something strange was occurring he later inquired at the shipyard if anyone had previously seen this figure on the bridge, but no one had. He then told them what he had seen and that the man had disappeared in seconds but, as could be expected, they all laughed at him.

A few weeks later one of his workmates (who had a reputation throughout the shipyard as being a 'hard man') told him that he had seen the same thing which he described previously and that it had also disappeared. Because of his reputation no one dared jest him on the matter and after this everyone who passed over the bridge began to look out for the figure, but without success. A few months later a member of the Harbour Police was on patrol at the quay side near the bridge late in the evening. He noticed a man (who was wearing a cloak) standing at the side on the bridge and knowing that he was 'up to something' he hid behind a corner and watched him. The man stood for around five minutes and then suddenly jumped over and into the water. The constable ran over to the river's edge and looked into the water but observed that there were no ripples in the water and that there had been no splash when the man had jumped in. A search was later carried out and nothing found and no body was ever discovered afterwards. As for the cloaked figure, no sightings were ever reported again.

Queen's Bridge.

Behind Bars

In Belfast at present there are a number of tours available which bring folk around what are meant to be Belfast's haunted spots, but sadly they are simply the result of someone's overactive imagination. One perfect example is that of the Belfast hangman who roams the streets looking for victims, but the slight historical downfall is that not only have there never been any Belfast hangmen, but there is no record of any Irish ones either! In Belfast there are thousands of ghost stories and for people such as myself, the hard work is not in gathering them but in trying to figure out which ones are absolute rubbish.

People do this in different ways but I do this by exploring the incident on which the ghost stories are based. For example, if it's centred on a man who was tragically killed in a certain place, then I try to find out if a man was indeed killed at that place in tragic circumstances. If not then it's obviously rubbish. But there's really one question which we must ask ourselves when it comes to ghosts and that is, what are they? There are many explanations for the existence of ghosts, ranging from trapped souls through to 'things' caught in time. The latter would actually seem quite sensible given the fact that not all ghosts are 'human'. For example, in London there is the case of a ghostly bus and in several parts of the country there are cases of ghostly trains with one being the infamous ghost train of South Armagh. However, these explanations only focus on sightings but what of other supernatural activities? Poltergeists are infamous, causing paranormal experiences in which objects, and sometimes people, are thrown around. And if that is not good enough, then how do we explain ghostly feelings, sounds and smells?

The latter would seem to be quite unusual but there are numerous cases of strange smells in areas where paranormal activity occurs. The human body is made up of five senses, if we ignore the alleged sixth sense. There are ghosts which can be seen, ghosts who can be felt, ghosts who can be heard, so why not ghosts that can be smelt? Taste is not ignored, as there are indeed cases of people who have experienced a foul taste in their mouths in places of paranormal activity.

In Belfast there are cases of householders being almost overcome with the smell of gas even though the supply, when checked, was fine. One such case was on the Crumlin Road, and when the history of the house was researched, it was discovered that two sisters had actually died in the very room where the smell was detected. Further research found that they had been overcome by gas fumes. Another case on the Crumlin Road occurred at the Belfast Prison. There are numerous ghost stories concerning this building, one being the tale of an American Jew who was hanged in the 1930s for a murder which he may not have committed. A ghostly

HAUNTED BELFAST

figure matching his description had been seen wandering the walkways of the prison wings, and most of the sightings were reported by the wardens.

A few years ago I was one of those who organised several tours of this prison. Everyone on the tour agreed that once they were in the execution cell, they were overcome by a sudden coldness, and this was before they even knew what the cell was. Another ghost in the prison was said to be that of a young boy who had horrifically committed suicide, as he was terrified of being whipped by the prison hangman. For years after this tragedy, it was said that the cries of a young boy could be heard in the dead of night, which must have been a scary experience for the other prisoners.

A few months before the outbreak of the First World War, two parents were locked up in the Belfast Prison while their children were being looked after by the grandmother in two small rented rooms at 29 Constance Street, in the Ballymacarrett area of the city. The grandmother, Matilda Roberts, worked in the Belfast Ropeworks and when she went to work Mrs Lowry,

A story is told in Belfast of a Belfast hangman who roams the streets in search of victims … despite the fact that there was never a Belfast, or even an Irish, hangman.

HAUNTED BELFAST

The Crumlin Road Prison.

from whom the rooms were rented, looked after the children and gave them their breakfast. On 28 January 1914, Ms Roberts went to work as normal leaving Mrs Lowry to get the children up and give them their breakfast, which she did. Mrs Lowry lit a small fire in the front room to give them some heat and, after leaving the eldest child, aged seven, in charge, left to do some shopping. A short time afterwards Anna Hamilton, who lived next door at number 27, heard the screams of children coming from next door. On rushing in she found George Roberts, who was aged three, in flames. She managed to get him down on the floor and put out the flames using a shawl. She then ripped off the burning clothes and sent the other children to get help. Medical help arrived and the young child was taken to the Ulster Hospital in Templemore Avenue and placed in one of the emergency beds.

Back in the Belfast Prison the parents were told nothing of this occurrence, as there was no way of communicating with them. In these days the prison was extremely strict and was divided into separate sections for men, women and children.

There was never any talking allowed between prisoners and visits were only arranged under exceptional circumstances. That evening the prisoners were locked in their cells at the usual time of around 6 p.m. and Mrs Roberts, like the rest of the prison, settled down to sleep as they were usually awakened around 5 a.m. the following morning. However, this night Mrs Roberts was to get no sleep whatsoever. Later in the night she was awakened by the sound of gentle crying and she recognised the crying as that of her youngest child George. Mrs Roberts later stated that the crying stopped, but the second it did the room was filled with the most disgusting burning smell, which lingered for a few moments and then completely disappeared. Mrs Roberts went into hysterics, believing something was seriously wrong. She banged and banged at the strong wooden door until a warden came along but he simply told her to shut up and get back to her bed. This had no effect and poor Mrs Roberts continued banging and clawing at the door in tears until she fell down with exhaustion.

The warden had reported this and the time of the incident was noted as 2.35 a.m. Back at the Ulster Hospital, the young boy died as a result of his horrific injuries. The time of death was noted as 2.30 a.m.

The Strange Haunting of John Street

John Street was the portion of road which connected Donegall Street to North Street. It was demolished during the construction of what is now Royal Avenue in the 1880s, with the present Telegraph and Central Library being two of the new buildings to occupy it. One section of the old street consisted of a row of small country type houses, one of which was derelict and boarded up for a number of years because it was said to have been haunted by the ghost of an elderly woman.

The residents of the street told of how the former occupants were terrified out of their home in the 1860s by a ghost who threw various items of pottery and furniture around the back downstairs room and that on one occasion it wrecked every item which sat in the yard. One of the families' children later claimed to have seen what appeared to have been an old woman walking up and down in the back room talking to herself. The young girl then stated that the woman completely disappeared before her eyes. The family fled the house and after doing so the owner boarded it up and it was never let again.

In May 1882 workmen were laying new pipes and sewers through the street and as they were digging the trenches for pipes one of them discovered what appeared to have been human bones. The police were called and the bones were later found to have been of an old woman and appeared to have lain buried for a number of years.

The bones were removed and buried in the Union Graveyard and the hauntings were never heard of again.

John Street.

The Disturbing Ghost of Glengyle

Glengyle House was a large Victorian mansion which stood on Windsor Avenue in South Belfast. For much of the latter part of the 1800s this house was the home of Robert Graham Glendinning, the Liberal Member of Parliament for North Antrim. Mr Glendinning was an extremely wealthy man and apart from owning his own weaving business he also held prominent positions in several other leading weaving companies.

He was born on 5 April 1844, his father being William Bell Glendinning of Brakagh, Co. Tyrone. Later in life Robert Glendinning married Elizabeth Harden and they both set up home in Glengyle House.

For the first few years Mr and Mrs Glendinning and their servants did not experience anything unusual in the house. However, this was to change after the death of Mrs Glendinning in 1883. Shortly after her death the housemaids at Glengyle began to report a number of strange incidents throughout the house. One of the first notable incidents occurred one evening when Mr Glendinning returned home late after a meeting. Earlier in the evening two of the housemaids were involved in preparing Mr Glendinning's bedroom which included the lighting of the fire. When the housemaids left the room everything was in order - the fire had caught and was burning well. When Mr Glendinning entered the bedroom the bedclothes were lying on the floor and the fire had not been lit. Mr Glendinning was furious and called for his head servant. When the servant arrived Mr Glendinning castigated him for the condition of the room and the servant stated that he would investigate the matter when the girls returned the following morning.

The next day the servant spoke to the housemaids about the bedroom and both of them swore that when they had left the room everything was in order and they had no idea of how the mess had happened. The servant told their story to Mr Glendinning and after a word of warning to the housemaids the matter was allowed to drop. This same incident occurred at least another three times and on one of these occasions the head servant himself saw that everything was in order and had personally locked the bedroom door to ensure that no one could enter the room. When the door was again opened an hour later it was discovered that the bedclothes were again disturbed and the fire had gone out. When the servant examined the fire he discovered that the coals were stone cold which would have been impossible even if the fire had gone out on its own accord. The head servant reported the incident to Mr Glendinning and confided that he believed something quite unusual was happening, but Mr Glendinning dismissed the whole matter as superstitious nonsense.

HAUNTED BELFAST

The servants and housemaids began to notice other strange happenings. These ranged from household objects being misplaced, to unusual noises being heard in numerous parts of the house. One of the objects which seemed to be moving of its own accord was a large vase which stood at the top of the central stairs. Mr Glendinning had informed the house staff to move this to another part of the hallway. A few days later Mr Glendinning asked why it had not been done and was told that the task had indeed been carried out by the head servant himself. When they went to check, the staff were shocked to see that the vase was back in its original position—it had not been there an hour previously. It was again moved and on this occasion Mr Glendinning watched but, to the disappointment of the servants, it remained at its new position. At this stage it seemed that these occurrences were directed at the house staff but this was soon to change

Every Sunday Mr Glendinning gave his servants and house staff the day off, as it was his strong religious belief that Sunday was a day of rest. Because of this the house staff prepared all the food on Saturday night and ensured that everything else throughout the house was in order. On Sunday evening Mr Glendinning was going to bed when he noticed a terrible smell in the upstairs corridor. On entering his bedroom he saw that his bedclothes were missing and that the curtains had been closed. When he left his bedroom that morning he had personally fixed his bed and had opened the curtains. When he went into the small washroom attached to his bedroom he noticed the bedclothes lying on the floor. Because he knew that there was no one else in the house he was mystified as to how this had happened. At first he thought that he had been burgled but when he saw that all the windows were shut and locked and that nothing was

Glengyle House.

Robert Glendinning.

missing, he soon dismissed this theory. Mr Glendinning now realised that this was no longer a case of 'superstitious nonsense' and the following morning he arranged a meeting to discuss the matter with all the house staff.

Everyone present had a different story to tell. As each person recounted their experience the group became uneasy. They all now suspected they were dealing with a 'paranormal' disturbance, but the question was, what was causing them? The only death to occur in the house recently was that of Mrs Glendinning. Had she returned to haunt Glengyle? Fortunately for Mr Glendinning and his house staff none of the incidents were serious and no injury was ever inflicted nor, it seemed, intended. Soon afterwards the incidents became few and far between and eventually they appeared to have stopped. Peace returned to Glengyle, for the time being.

A few years after the death of Mrs Glendinning, Robert Glendinning became acquainted with William Hastings through a number of business arrangements. Soon he became a close family friend and a number of years later Mr Glendinning was permitted to marry Mr Hasting's daughter Mary. Mr Glendinning had once again settled into family life but, unknown to him, it was not to be a peaceful one.

A few weeks after his second marriage the supernatural activity of years before reoccurred and once again the servants appeared to be the target of the disturbances. In addition to what had occurred previously, bells which summoned the servants to various parts of the house began to ring of their own accord and create a general confusion throughout the house. Items once again began to disappear and reappear a few days later. On one occasion, when the bells were again ringing, two of the housemaids left, vowing never to return. Mr Glendinning himself was subjected to some of the more disturbing aspects of the activity.

On numerous occasions in the middle of the night, smashing sounds were heard in the outside hallway but when it was investigated everything was in order and nothing had been broken. Often there would be very loud banging on the bedroom door and when this occurred, Mr and the new Mrs Glendinning were often so terrified that they would not leave the bedroom. Eventually, Mr Glendinning and his new wife went to live in another part of Belfast with his brother. Arrangements were made for them to stay there for a short time while they found somewhere else to live. However, nothing suitable was found and they reluctantly moved back to Glengyle.

When they did return they were informed by the house staff that there had been no additional incidents since in their absence. Mr Glendinning was now convinced that these hauntings were connected to the death of his first wife but was totally bewildered as to why they were happening. The incidents reoccurred and this time the strange smell reappeared, as did 'crackling' noises in the front reception room.

By the turn of the last century the incidents had only increased in frequency and Mr Glendinning was forced to move to a new house beside one of his brothers, in the university area. He, his wife, and house staff moved to 'Knock-Dhu' which was situated at 41 Sans Souci Park off the University Road. Here there was no paranormal activity and the new occupants of Glengyle reported that nothing unusual occurred while they lived there.

It appeared that all the strange behaviour was at an end, and right up until Mr Glendinning's death in the mid 1920s, there were no further incidents reported. Why these incidents occurred in the first place still remains a total mystery.

The Ghosts of
the Lord Kelvin

In the Victorian period, and for many decades in the last century, fire was a major threat to anyone who owned property or lived in a house. The main reason for this was the fact that buildings had no fire escapes, alarms or sprinkler systems and the fire brigade of the time had nothing like the capability of today's service.

During this period there were thousands of fires and many of them resulted in a loss of life. If we look through the old newspapers of the Victorian era we can see exactly what kind of threat fire posed. A serious fire with loss of life was almost a weekly occurrence in Belfast and many other parts of Ireland.

After the fires in which people died, stories would begin to circulate stating that ghostly figures had been seen among the ruins and that sometimes ghastly screams could be heard. Needless to say, many of the stories were untrue but there were exceptions.

There are a few local examples. One of these was the incident which occurred in connection with the Lucifer Match Factory, and which is told elsewhere in this book. Another is the story in which the ghostly apparition of a fireman was seen by different people on the site of an old flour mill on the Falls Road. In December 1882 a large fire destroyed Hughes Flour Mill and the fire brigade in Townhall Street were sent for. The building, which was situated between Alexander Street West and Gilford Street, was eight stories high, and when the firemen arrived it was mainly the upper sections which were ablaze. Some hours later the fire brigade got the blaze under control and water was being poured on the small burning sections, when a large wall crashed down on top of them. One of the firemen, Samuel Patterson, was killed instantly, his head literally being crushed to a pulp. Others were taken to the Royal Hospital in Frederick Street including the dead man's brother and James Doherty, who died a few days later.

The following year, after the site was cleared and reconstruction work began, a number of people reported seeing a fireman walking around the site. No one claimed to have seen it up close but most claimed that the man disappeared before their eyes. As was usual in those days, considerable excitement ensued and many people went to the area in the hope of catching a glimpse. On one occasion a crowd had gathered after the figure of a man was seen walking into one of the buildings, but they were disappointed to learn that the sighting was nothing more than a patrolling watchman. As usual, interest soon died away and there were claims of additional sightings, but when the construction work ended so did the sightings. Believing that this was a 'seasonal ghost' a group of people gathered at the site in December 1884 but nothing out of the ordinary was seen or heard and eventually the story died away.

The lounge of the Lord Kelvin, where the fire originated.

The Kelvin Hotel was situated in College Square East. It was named after the world famous scientist Lord Kelvin, who was born in the building when it was a private house. In the early hours of Tuesday 26 July 1910, a small fire broke out in the lounge. This was situated at the bottom of a spiral staircase which led to all the corridors of the building. When the fire was discovered it had reached halfway up the stairs, making escape by this route impossible. As previously stated, buildings at this time did not have fire escapes and many of the hotel's guests made their escape through the lower windows into the safety of the street but others, whose quarters were in the upper floors, found themselves in the dilemma of choosing to burn in the building or jump from the windows. Among those who faced this impossible choice was the Rev. McCaughan, minister of the May Street Presbyterian Church, who was staying in the hotel along with his wife. Both stood on the window of the second floor and Mrs McCaughan was the first to leap on to the street below. She was seriously injured and was immediately rushed to hospital. Her husband paused and when the flames began to get closer he decided to leap. At the front of the building large iron letters reading 'Kelvin Hotel' were placed along the front of the building. The minister's foot caught on the letter 'H' and he therefore hit the ground head first. Like his wife, he was seriously injured and taken straight to hospital. Both died a few days later.

In a separate incident two hotel porters were trapped in an upstairs room after they had been banging doors getting everyone up. They tried to breakout through the roof but were overcome by fumes and suffocated.

The Lord Kelvin, after the fire.

The Reverend McCaughey who jumped from his window at the Lord Kelvin to escape the flames.

The rear of the hotel. It was below this roof that two porters met their deaths.

Many of the hotel's guests found a safe escape route at the rear of the building by climbing through a window and jumping onto a flat roof and then travelling down along the back entry. A man named Fred Cosset (a commercial traveller from Stockport) hesitated too long before jumping—when he decided to do so the fire had weakened the roof underneath, causing him to crash through it into the flames below. His charred body was discovered later as were those of another man who was never identified.

This tragedy was one of the worst fire disasters ever witnessed in Belfast. A few days later the salvage unit of the Belfast Fire Brigade moved in to make sure the remains of the building were safe. During this work, one of the men reported hearing coughing sounds coming from some of the surviving rooms but after an extensive search nothing was found. The hotel never reopened and the remains of the building were converted into a picture house. When this establishment opened many of the people who worked there began to report sightings and various unexplained sounds such as coughing, moaning and distant screams. The main sightings seemed to be the faint apparition of a man who was seen in the store rooms at the back of the screen. Two of these sightings were reported by the owner himself. The sightings continued right up until the building was converted into the Mayfair Theatre and until its demolition. New office blocks occupy the site today but, to date, it is unknown if there have been any modern sightings.

The Ghost of the University

The commercial centre of Belfast has many stories of hauntings in the old city centre buildings. One of these stories centres on a tragic event in High Street which was instantly connected to an eerie sighting in the south of the city.

In 1890 Margaret McCullough lived at No.126 University Street. At this time the street was regarded as a 'high class' thoroughfare and many of the city's wealthy merchants and lecturers lived here. No.126 was a large house which contained many bedrooms and because Margaret McCullough lived alone, she quite often let out rooms to carefully selected lodgers. All of those who lodged in this landlady's premises had to follow a very strict set of rules and the main one was that they must be employed. During their working hours they were not permitted into the house and the only exception to this rule was illness. One of these lodgers at this time was nineteen year old Arthur Taylor who had come to Belfast from Sligo. He served his apprenticeship in his father's carpet establishment and in 1889 he came to Belfast, one year after it was made a city. He was employed in J.C. Mayre's carpet warehouse in Royal Avenue. Arthur hated this job as he was often the victim of sectarian remarks.

On Friday 14 March 1890, he obtained for himself another job, this time in Hanna & Browne House Furnishers, in High Street. He was to start the following Monday (24 March 1890) and was delighted to be out of Mayre's. That week he had been restless as he was looking forward to his new job, and when the Monday finally arrived he was up earlier than usual as he wished to walk to his new employment.

When all the lodgers were out of the house Miss McCullough began her usual routine of cleaning. As she was polishing the woodwork in the hallway she noticed Arthur coming up the stairs. She called to him but he ignored her. She rushed down but when she reached the landing she noticed that there was no sign of him. She knocked on his bedroom door but there was no answer. Suspecting that something was wrong she immediately went down to her own quarters and fetched the key to Arthur's room. When she let herself in she was shocked to discover that the room was empty. The landlady was totally mystified as to where the young gentleman could have disappeared. She recorded in her notebook and that she had entered Arthur's room at 9.10 a.m.

Arthur had started his new job at 7.30 a.m. He was shown around the premises and afterwards told to compile a full check on all their 'lino' rolls and rugs. The rolls were placed in large shelves situated on the second floor. At the top of these all the rugs were kept. After checking the rolls he began to count the rugs and to do this he had to stand on a small step ladder. As he was doing so, he lost his footing and fell. He attempted to prevent his fall by gripping one of the shelves but instead his hand reached one of the rolls. His attempt to stop his fall failed and resulted only in bringing one of the heavy rolls down on top of himself. Arthur received a serious head wound and died a short time afterwards. Hanna & Browne immediately closed their shop and it remained closed for the entire day. That evening an inquest was held in the premises and the details were recorded.

> On Monday 17 March 1890, at a quarter to five o'clock, Dr Dill, city coroner, and a respectable jury held an inquest on the body of Arthur Taylor in one of the rooms of the carpet department of Messrs. Hanna & Browne's warehouse. Head Constable Funston watched the proceedings on behalf of the constabulary, and Mr. J. R. Moorhead, solicitor, appeared for Messrs. Hanna & Browne. Mr. J. Taylor, Sligo, father of the deceased, arrived shortly after five o'clock. Mr. S. McCullough was sworn, and identified the body as that of Arthur Taylor, who was about eighteen years of age and unmarried. He was previously employed in the establishment of Mr. J. C. Mayres, and left it about eight day's ago. Alexander Smith, 48 Beverley Street, who is in the employment of Messrs. Hanna & Browne, said that he was coming upstairs on Monday morning to the second flight, and when within a few steps from the top saw the deceased on a stepladder. When he was coming down the ladder, instead of putting his foot on the step in front, he put it over the ladder, where there was no step, thereby overbalancing himself and falling from a height of about four feet. He fell on his back, and when falling caught hold of a roll of linoleum, which, being loose, came with him and fell on his forehead. Witness went to his assistance and lifted the deceased up, the linoleum having rolled off his body. He then laid deceased on the floor on a carpet and went for a doctor. The deceased was unconscious until his death.
> Mr. Morehead – 'Were the ladders at all broken?'
> Witness – 'The rails on the back of the ladder were broken by the deceased in his fall.'

Mr R Symmonds, 47 Willowfield Street, deposed to seeing the deceased on the ladder looking at some mats. He had his back to him, when he heard a slight noise, and on looking round saw the deceased lying on the floor on his back. The doctor was then sent for. Mr James Brown, 39 Lonsdale Street, one of the partners of the firm, deposed that he saw the deceased on the premises at eight o'clock on Monday morning. He told him he wanted him to go to the carpet department and the deceased said he was willing to go any place. Witness then told the deceased to look at the stock, and became acquainted with it. He left him with Mr Symmonds. A short time afterwards one of the young men came to witness in the top story of the house and said that an accident had occurred in the carpet department, and he came down at once. He saw Arthur Taylor lying on the floor, and, observing that it was serious, asked if a doctor had been sent for. A lad had already been dispatched for one, and witness went for Dr Speer, who immediately drove over to the place and examined the deceased. Witness was not aware that deceased had any reason for leaving Mr Mayre's employment further than he wished a new situation.
A Juror – 'Has there been any accidents prior to this?'
Witness – 'There has never been an accident in the place before.'
  Mr Taylor stated that his son had been in Belfast since May 1889. He had served part of his apprenticeship in witness's own establishment in Sligo, and came to Belfast to follow the same business. He recently wrote to the witness to the effect that he wished to leave the establishment he was then in, and witness replied that he was glad he had got another situation in the city. Witness was quite satisfied that the steps used by him were safe, and had no fault to find with them.

High Street, where Arthur Taylor worked.

Arthur came from Sligo to work in Belfast.

Dr Speer deposed that he was called about nine o'clock to see the deceased, who was at that time just expiring, there being only the slightest signs of breathing. Blood was coming from his mouth and left ear. The cause of death was fracture of the base of the skull, accelerated by a large venous injury near the said fracture.

After hearing all the evidence the jury returned a verdict of death from injuries accidentally received. The inquest then recorded the details and the time of death was recorded as 9.00 a.m.

The Infamous Galloper Thompson

All of us know some sort of ghost story, but there is no doubt that many of the stories which we were told in our childhood were nothing but mere fiction, the result of someone's overactive imagination. Unfortunately when it comes to ghost stories the boundaries between fact and fiction are never very clear. Many of us, when told a fictitious story, were so terrified as children that the story stuck with us and eventually we believed it. Then there was the problem with the 'additions'—someone would tell a story and when it was repeated, various bits and pieces would be added on to enhance the story. This could go on and on until the final story is nothing like the original.

One ghost story to which this has happened is the famous Belfast tale of 'Galloper Thompson.' There are numerous stories surrounding this ghost and from the 'bits added on' it appears his story made the rounds. The basic story was centred on Gordon Thompson, an eccentric character who travelled around the world. When he returned home he settled into a house in Upper Donegall Street. A few years later he began to build a house on the Crumlin Road. When he moved there in 1851, he named the building 'Bedeque House.' The house he had just built was modelled on a property on Prince Edward Island. Thompson lived here until 1872 when he sold the house to Frederick Kinahan, who in turn later sold it to the Catholic Church, who then used it as a new hospital. They later demolished the house and the site is today occupied by the Mater Hospital. But who, or what, was this 'Galloper Thompson?'

Gordon Augustus Thompson was of the old family of Thompson's of Castleton, or Jennymount. Third son of John Thompson, one of the original directors of the Belfast Banking Company, he went to live with relatives called Gordon—West India merchants, one of whom was the Governor of Montserrat. Thompson's mother, Anne Wilson, was of the same family as Walter Wilson, shipbuilder. A faint idea of his wandering moods is gathered from the description of his having camped on part of the ground now covered by Melbourne. An early letter writer confirms the suggestion. 'Gordon Thompson', said a Wilson of Maryville, 'returned to Belfast after twelve years travel. He came to Maryville one day every week and delighted us all with his stories of the Rocky Mountains, Andes. etc.' He was a member of the Belfast Town Council in 1849, and for a few years afterwards. In response to the call of the wild, he returned to Australia and died in Melbourne in 1886 at the age of eighty-seven. His portrait in oils was in the Municipal Art Gallery. There is an appropriate 'Fenimore Cooperesque' flavour about his monumental inscription in Carnmoney, 'The last of the family name - Thompson's of Jennymount.'

Bedeque House.

The Castleton Thompson's were best known as bankers, of whom there were three generations. Robert (1736-1800) of Jennymount; John (1766-1824) of Jennymount; and John (1798-1874) of Lowwood. The first John had three sons: Robert of Castleton (1792-1862); John of Lowwood; and Gordon Augustus of Bedeque House. He was one of the founders of the Commercial Bank (1809) which, by amalgamation with the Belfast Bank, subsequently became the Belfast Banking Company. Both father and (second) son were, in succession, the head directors of this concern. The elder Robert Thompson, grandfather of Gordon, was principal partner in the earlier Discount Company, and was probably the first occupant of Jennymount, called, it is believed, after his sister. Their father was John Thompson (1691-1765), Presbyterian minister of Carnmoney for thirty-four years and their mother was Jane Legg, of Malone House.

The Rev. John Thompson was succeeded in the ministry of the same church by his nephew, also John Thompson, a man of very decided character and great influence during his sixty-two years of active duty. He was a native of Shilvodan, near Connor, and it was probably here that the family settled originally in the seventeenth century. His sons Charles and William were well-known merchants in High Street, their mother being the daughter of the Rev. William Laird of Rosemary Street, and they were succeeded by their nephews, the Finlays. Sir Thomas McClure was also a grandson of the Carnmoney minister, and joined the Finlays in a business which later became the Wolfhill Spinning Company. Among the family papers is a document (with seal)

High Street.

dated 1703, certifying that, 'Mr. John Thompson, preacher of the Gospel, was admitted a burgess of the Burgh of Irvine in Scotland', which may give some clue to the source of the family.

As in many old houses, popular superstition attributed a banshee to the Jennymount residence; and in the legendary lore of Ireland 'Galloper Thompson' has found a place.

We now know who Galloper Thompson was, and who his family were, but what exactly is the story connected with this ghostly rider?

There is no doubt that the tale of Galloper Thompson is the most famous of all Belfast ghost stories. The story began when Gordon Thompson stated to his friends that when he died, if he did not find a place in heaven, he would return and haunt Jennymount. A few years after his death a number of people reported seeing the ghostly apparition of a man riding a horse at breakneck speed along old Jennymount Avenue. As Gordon Thompson rode a horse at speed almost daily, many stated that it was his ghost. It was this activity which gave Gordon Thompson the name 'Galloper'. The story continues today and when Jennymount was demolished, it was claimed that the apparition could be seen in the area around Alexandra Park Avenue, which replaced Jennymount Drive.

Needless to say because of the fact that this is a Victorian story it has been told so many times that 'additions' have been added. In the story itself there are those who claimed to have been almost knocked over by the speeding horse and rider, while others claimed that neither had any heads.

Jennymount.

There was also another story added which stated that Galloper often went to the stables of a nearby house to take a horse out for a ride. He would then return the horse and the following day the owners would be totally mystified as to how the horse got into such a dirty state. The story was often used by parents to scare their children to come in early and go to bed. Many people continue to remember their mothers and fathers telling them to be in for a certain time or 'Galloper Thompson will get ye'. We can now wonder if the children ever got to sleep after being frightened with such a tale?

Because the story was based in North Belfast, it left other areas at a disadvantage when it came to discipline. Often the tale of Galloper was used in the same way with the only difference being that he had moved to the area where the story was being told. Another 'addition' to the story was a new ending. Some people heard that a minister had tricked Galloper Thompson into a bottle. He then handed the bottle to a sailor who dumped it into the Red Sea. However, where this occurred or how it happened was never made clear.

Like all ghost stories no one can say if the tale of Galloper Thompson is true or not, but what is fact is that it is a fascinating story and that the 'real' Galloper Thompson was one of the most extraordinary characters Belfast has ever known.

Jubbie the Tram Chaser

When we think of ghosts we think of everything from banshees to a white sheet with two holes in it, but on most occasions they are in some sort of human form. Of all the ghosts, not many have been reported as cats, dogs, horses, wolves or various farmyard creatures.

Throughout Ireland there are actually thousands of such cases with the most famous being the phantom black dogs which are said to roam the hills and mountains in the west of the country. Belfast is no exception and it is believed that the last wolf in Ireland was killed in the Ligoneil area, and that it can still be seen in the surrounding countryside.

Another story involving an animal haunting is about a small terrier dog called 'Jubbie.' Although this story does not have the romance of Irish legend which surrounds the Ligoneil wolf, it is still a fascinating tale.

At the turn of the last century Jubbie and his owner were a very famous pair throughout the Shankill Road area, as Jubbie had a terrible habit of chasing trams. Every day his owner, an elderly gentleman who lived in Mayo Street, would walk Jubbie up to the Woodvale Park and release him from his lead. Most days this was a normal occurrence and Jubbie would then run around and play with the other dogs.

However, if a tram was passing, Jubbie would rush out and chase it. The owner, filled with embarrassment, would then put the lead in his pocket and walk on, pretending that the dog was not his. Jubbie would then run around the tram and constantly bark at its wheels until it stopped and the conductor chased him away. It would then go back to the entrance of the park and sit and wait on his owner to collect him on his way out. It was because of this that the pair was known to everyone in the area.

One rainy day the two set off as usual for their walk in the park and after being released from his lead Jubbie was off in his personal war against trams and as usual the dog's master walked on with the lead in his pocket. Jubbie ran around the tram as usual but this time it did not stop as it was running late. Jubbie ran under the tram and was cut in half by the tram's wheels, being killed instantly. The tram was stopped and the conductor got off. After picking up the dog's remains he carefully set them down at the side of the road. Those on board later stated that he had tears in his eyes, something which would be easily believed, as Jubbie was known to every tram conductor and driver who ever travelled up the Shankill Road. When the owner returned to the park gate and saw no sign of Jubbie he stood and waited on him to come back. As he was waiting he was approached by a woman who told him that his 'wee' dog was lying dead further down the road and that it had been run over by a tram. The old man picked up the remains

A Belfast tram.

and took them home, the blood from his dog soaking into his clothes. Those who were walking towards him stood to one side to allow him to pass.

In the days and weeks which followed there was no sign of the man and many people believed that he would not come out as his only companion was now dead. Reports now began to circulate about people seeing Jubbie waiting at the park's entrance as though it were waiting on its master. Hundreds of people claimed to have seen it and all reported the same thing: a small dog sitting on the footpath at the entrance of Woodvale Park. A few more weeks had passed but no one had seen any sign of the old man. His neighbours were very concerned. The police were informed and, after a constable forced an entrance to the man's house, he was found dead, sitting on a chair with the decomposed remains of Jubbie on his lap. When the man returned home after the dog's death he had just sat on the chair and not moved for either food or water. Neighbours believed that he died of a broken heart. After this, no sightings of the ghostly dog were ever reported again. It seems that Jubbie's wait for his master to collect him was over.

A Sandy Row Ghost Story

One of the most historic areas of Belfast is that known as Sandy Row. This old district is almost as old as the town of Belfast itself and when the town began to grow and prosper Sandy Row came into existence as a thoroughfare for traders bringing their goods to the markets in the south and west and to Belfast itself. One of the main commercial goods at the time was cotton and many hand-loom weavers worked their small cotton looms in thatched cottages in Sandy Row, so that they could sell their wares to the many traders passing through. Another commodity which was sold in Belfast was water and all the barrels which were sold in Fountain Street were filled at a natural spring situated in Sandy Row. This was known as 'Monday's Well.'

In the latter part of the 1700s Sandy Row began to become more of an industrial district. This really began in 1783 when a new brickwork business was established in the area. This 'industrialisation' was to continue over the next one hundred years and reached its peak when Murphy & Stephenson built a number of cheap houses for their mill workers. Before the town of Belfast became a city in 1888, the town was described as being made up of a number of small villages; Sandy Row was listed as one of them.

Due to its rich history, it would be expected that this small area would have an abundance of ghost stories. It does, and no period produced more than the turn of the last century. One of the most popular stories at that time was the Victorian tale about the ghost of 'Old Corby'.

In 1879 a coal porter named James Aitchison and his family moved into number 60 Sandy Row. When they first moved in, the family immediately noticed that there was an 'uneasy' feeling to this house but they put this down to being in a strange environment. However, after settling in they experienced a number of strange incidents. Their eight-year-old daughter slept in a back room upstairs and occasionally she would wake up in the middle of the night screaming. When her parents rushed in she would be sitting up in her bed crying that she had seen a strange man in her bedroom. At first her parents put this down to nightmares, but when it happened more often the child was taken out of this room and placed in her parent's bedroom. The room remained empty for the duration of the family's stay here and no additional incidents occurred.

The Aitchison family moved elsewhere and the house was occupied by a labourer named Lowry. One day Mr Lowry was carrying out repairs in his backyard when he noticed an elderly man standing at the bottom of his ladder. He called down to the man but received no reply. When he started down the ladder the man disappeared before Lowry's eyes. Lowry was petrified, and after stumbling down the ladder he rushed out of the house and into the street.

Old Corby hung himself in the backyard of this house.

He immediately went to a local clergyman and explained to him what had just occurred. The clergyman then told Mr Lowry of previous incidents connected with this house, and what he believed was causing them. The clergyman, instead of reassuring Mr Lowry, appeared to have terrified the man even more. The labourer refused to go anywhere near the house after their talk. After this incident no one else moved to the house. It was believed throughout the district that the property was haunted by the ghost of 'Old Corby.'

The house lay derelict for a number of years after this and at the turn of the century it was bought and converted to a hairdressing salon by the Ashwood family. As the conversion work was being carried out some of the workmen reported seeing the figure of a man in the backyard, but when they went out to investigate no one was there. This occurred a few times and when the locals told them the story connected with the house, they treated the matter with a great deal of humour. The story came to the attention of the Ashwood family who dismissed it as foolishness. After the family set up their hairdressing business, they began to hear of sightings of this old man and on several occasions family members themselves actually saw the figure. The family came to accept the story as being true but as they continued in their business the sightings became less frequent, before stopping completely.

As stated this ghost was known in the locality as 'Old Corby.' But who was 'Old Corby' and what was the story behind the sightings? Because no one actually knew the full story quite a few myths became connected with the tale. The most popular was that 'Old Corby' was a dealer who lived in the house some years previous and who had been mysteriously murdered. Nothing could be further from the truth.

Much of the water sold throughout the Belfast was from a spring at Sandy Row.

'Old Corby' was a seventy-seven year old man named Corbett who had lived in the house for much of the last century. Mr Corbett was said to be 'doating' and became very well known throughout Sandy Row due to his unusual behaviour. Mr Corbett lived in this house with his son, the housekeeper Mrs Moore, and her son. All those occupying the house worked and Mr Corbett was often left in the house alone. On Friday 11 February 1876 Mrs Moore's son returned from work and as he was sitting down for a meal asked where his seat was. His mother replied that Mr Corbett had taken it out into the backyard earlier to do something, and that it must still be out there. Moore went out to search for the chair and saw it lying at the backyard wall. He then found Mr Corbett hanging inside an enclave on a crook in the wall. Needless to say, the boy was horrified and rushed back into the house. After the inquest, held the following morning, it was discovered that the old man had committed suicide and that he had been of unsound mind at the time. After the tragedy the occupants of number 61 moved out and were followed by the Aitchison's. It was then that the sightings began.

The Ghost of Ballymacarrett

Many the strange tale of the supernatural has been told at a Belfast fireside and indeed the tradition of passing such ghost stories from generation to generation has been a strong one throughout the country. Such a story was related to me recently by a man who still lives in the east of the city: the scene of the haunting. The story was handed down to him from his father, who told him that the facts are authentic as they were experienced by his own father who was a signalman on the County Down Railway.

The story is set at the turn of the present century and it was reputedly a twice-yearly occurrence in the city. One November evening the fog was so dense that you could barely see in front of you. The street lights were the only form of guidance you had to help steer you homewards through the winding streets of Ballymacarrett. The 7.30 Bangor train had just passed by the signal box opposite Central Street when the signal-man's shift ended for the night. It was a lonely job and as he climbed down the steps onto the siding, he was glad to be leaving. It was a terrible night so he was looking forward to having a few bottles of stout at the pub before going home to the wife and kids. With this in mind he held his lantern before him and tried to make his way back to the station along the tracks.

At that moment he heard someone not far behind him. A shiver went up his back. Who on earth would be coming down the tracks on such a night? He stopped and waited and eventually he could make out the figure of a woman approaching him through the fog. She was a woman in her late twenties and as she got nearer she greeted him: 'Thank God you waited on me, it's a terrible night. You can hardly see two feet in front of ye!' she said. The two of them headed back to the station together. On the way the young woman explained that she had been taking a shortcut to the city centre where she was going to meet her cousin.

When they eventually reached the station he led her through and bade the woman good night before signing himself out. His shift was finished for the night and as he walked out onto Station Street, a sinister feeling came over him again. The fog was still as thick as it had been earlier and very few people were wandering about the streets. Not that you could have seen them anyway. As he walked towards Memel Street he could hear the kids playing 'rally-o'. He could barely make out the flickering gas lights as he headed towards the Aero Bar on Bridge End. The yarns his granny used to tell him about the ghosts at the Lagan and even the strange stories about the banshee on the yard wall began to torment his mind. As he walked on towards the pub he tried to convince himself that there was no such thing and anyway he was a full-grown man, he shouldn't be worried by such nonsense. Even so, he was still feeling anxious.

Soon he could hear singing and the lights of the pub became clearer and clearer. In through the doors he went and straight up to the bar. A couple of other railway workers were there before him. He got a bottle of stout and joined their company. As they got talking, he told them of the woman he met that night on the tracks and how terrible a night it had been. 'Who was she?' one of the company asked. 'She said her name was Harvey or something like that', he replied. He couldn't remember her first name but he tried to explain what she looked like: thin build, straight red hair, in her late twenties.

Then someone interrupted. 'Are you sure her name was Harvey?' The elderly man who asked the question then told his captive audience about an incident which took place in that area in 1896.

In February of that year a ghastly discovery was made on the Holywood branch of the County Down Railway, adjacent to the Ballymacarrett signal station, by a local man who had been returning from his post on the night shift. As he was walking down the line he stumbled upon the mutilated remains of a woman lying scattered over the rails at the junction where the Bangor and Holywood line separates. The newspapers recorded the spectacle as being 'sickening in the extreme.' The body, which was lying between the lines, was completely severed in two, and portions of it were scattered for a distance of fifty yards, 'the place all round being saturated with blood'. Sergeant Gough from Mountpottinger Road Barracks was one of the first on the scene.

Under his direction, the pieces of the body were gathered up and removed to the morgue. Later in the day the body was identified as that of Catherine Hanvey. She had been a single woman of around thirty years of age who had worked as a domestic servant in a house on the Lisburn Road. She had been living with her sister at Montrose Street when she left to visit some friends at Holywood. When her body was discovered, a punched third-class railway ticket from Belfast to Holywood was found in her pocket, indicating that she had been on board the train. The date was also printed on the ticket and the cause of that evening's tragic event gradually became clearer. One way or another she had fallen from the carriage of the train and as her body lay on the tracks it had been passed over and knocked about by a number of different trains.

Ballymacarrett Railway Station.

Subsequent inquest evidence tried to ascertain whether she had been of unsound mind and therefore if she fell from the train by accident, or she jumped in an attempt at suicide. To this very day we do not know for sure. Upon further enquiries we turned up the inquest verdict to the horrific death. The verdict was as follows:

> That the said Catherine Hanvey, on the 21st February 1896, on the Holywood and Bangor branch of the Belfast and County Down Railway, opposite Central Street, Ballymacarrett, in the City of Belfast, came to her death from injuries received, caused by an engine and train passing over her.

The signal man dismissed the whole thing as nonsense. He finished up his stout and told the company he'd have to head home to the 'missus.' He took out his pocket-watch to see how late he was. It had stopped, at 7.30 p.m.

The Victoria Barracks

One part of the city of Belfast which has had 'ghosts galore' was the old Victoria military establishment which stood in North Queen Street in the north of the city. These old barracks dated back to the 1790s and there is no doubt that many thousands of troops served within the complex up until its demolition in the 1960s. Many tales were told in the old barrack rooms to pass in the countless boring nights and, as could be expected, ghost stories played a major part in the 'story-tellers' narration. A great part of these stories was undoubtedly the result of an active imagination, however other stories could not be dismissed as pure fantasy and the barracks themselves had many paranormal stories connected with them.

A great number of these military ghosts appear to be centred on suicides which occurred during various periods of the establishment's long history and which were committed by depressed soldiers who were far away from home. Other 'ghosts' are connected with deaths that occurred in mysterious circumstances such as the many murders committed during the Luftwaffe blitz of 1941. What is clear is that all the ghosts of Victoria Barracks are connected with tragic deaths within that complex. There is a single well-documented supernatural incident connected with the old barracks which is among the strangest of all Irish ghost stories. Technically speaking it is more a case of paranormal phenomenon than a ghost story as no ghost was actually seen. As stated, the incident is well documented in historical records and the reason for this is due to the fact that there were so many witnesses and that the event caused widespread excitement throughout the base.

Shortly after nine o'clock on the morning of Thursday 28 October 1909, detachments of the D & G Companies of the Cheshire Regiment left Victoria Barracks under the command of Captain Rich and Captain Tahourdin. They were going to the banks of the River Lagan in order to carry out a bridging and raft building exercise. They arrived at a stretch of the river below the first lock at Ballynafeigh and once there they started their operations. Both officers and men had considerable practice at constructing a raft, and in a very short time several large barrels, which formed the foundation of the pontoon, were tied together, with planks laid across the top of them. In the meantime five soldiers had rowed to the other side and placed a rope across the river which was to be used to haul the pontoon across.

When the first raft was constructed it was tested with a few men on it. When it had returned from the opposite bank it was decided to test it with a much heavier load. Nearly thirty men were placed on it with the rest of the detachment remaining on shore to finish the construction of a second raft. By this stage a large group of spectators had gathered to watch the activities of the troops and when the raft began to be pulled across there was amazement at how it was still afloat. The crowd cheered and clapped the success of the soldiers. Once the craft was about fifteen yards from the bank, and in deep water, it lurched suddenly. There was a confused moment among the soldiers as they tried to balance the weight out but suddenly, and without warning, the whole pontoon up-ended and turned clean over. The assembled crowd became hysterical with laughter but this soon changed to concern when it became clear that things were not as they should have been. Some of the men managed to jump clear of the over-turned craft and swim for the bank. Others sank and came up clinging to barrels and planks while others appeared to go down with the weight of the remaining sections of the pontoon on top of them. There was wild confusion and some troops jumped into the only boat to go out and offer assistance. This was a disaster as the boat was soon swamped by the men in the water and overturned. Some of the assembled crowd at one side (Stranmillis) waded out and helped some of the men who could not swim, into the safety of shallow water.

The people of the neighbourhood provided every assistance possible by supplying hot drinks and dry clothing. As soon as the confusion subsided and the last of the soldiers had been pulled ashore the roll was called. It was then discovered that two men, Lance Sergeant Fitzpatrick and Private Whelan, had not answered their names, and that there had been no sign of them on the opposite bank. The two unaccounted men were among the best swimmers in the regiment and it was first thought that they may have swum a distance in the confusion. A search was immediately launched and when this failed to discover any trace of the two men it was assumed that they had gone down with the raft.

Medical assistance was summoned and Dr Nathaniel McConnell arrived speedily on the scene, followed a short time afterwards by a party of the Medical Corps. More troops arrived and dredging operations begun at once. A few hours later this operation uncovered the dead body of Sergeant Fitzpatrick. Major Todd was in command and he ordered the troops to continue the search until the other body was found. Later that night, the body of Private Whelan was also found. He had a cut on his forehead and from this it was assumed that he had been struck by the raft and knocked out, his body then being carried off by an underwater current.

On Monday 1 November 1909, an inquest was held in Victoria Barracks into the two deaths. The City Coroner, Dr James Graham, and a jury, recorded that the whole affair was a tragic accident and returned the following verdict: that Private William Whelan and Lance Sergeant John Fitzpatrick, on the 28 October 1909, near the first locks on the River Lagan, were accidentally drowned by being thrown from a raft, constructed by a detachment of the Cheshire Regiment under the command of Captain Tahoundin for drill purposes, which capsized same time and place from some unknown cause.

After the inquest the military kits of the two dead men were removed from their bunks and placed into storage. What the inquest failed to mention, but which the army records did, were the strange events which began to occur soon after the tragedy. On the night of Friday 29 November a large number of troops were in their bunks within the barrack quarters. A few minutes before eleven o'clock, one of the soldiers felt the sides of his bunk being squeezed in. Believing that someone was under his bed playing a prank, he waited to see what was going to happen, planning to then catch the prankster. The squeezing continued for a few minutes and when it stopped the soldier reached under the bed and was startled to discover that there was no one there. He had figured that it was impossible for anyone to have escaped from under his bed without being detected. This mystified him and the following day when he was discussing it with others he was shocked to discover that he was not alone in his experience.

It was revealed that during the night a number of the other soldiers had felt the same thing. All those who had experienced this strange occurrence had been totally mystified at what had caused it, but as the day progressed a startling discovery was made as more soldiers in the camp heard the stories.

One of the men who died in the previous day's accident had been a practical joker. Private Whelan was well known to the rest of his regiment for carrying out various pranks and one which he was well known for involved the tucking in of blankets. What Private Whelan did was wait until one of the regiment's heavier sleepers drifted off and remove the blanket from the top of their bunk. The arms of the 'victim' were then placed down by their sides and the blanket tucked into the bed as tightly as possible. When this was done, Private Whelan would return to his bunk where he would have various bits and pieces to throw at the unfortunate sleeper. When the man awoke after being struck by an item, such as an old apple, he found that he was trapped in his own bed. All those who had the experience the previous night had fallen victim to this prank when Private Whelan was alive.

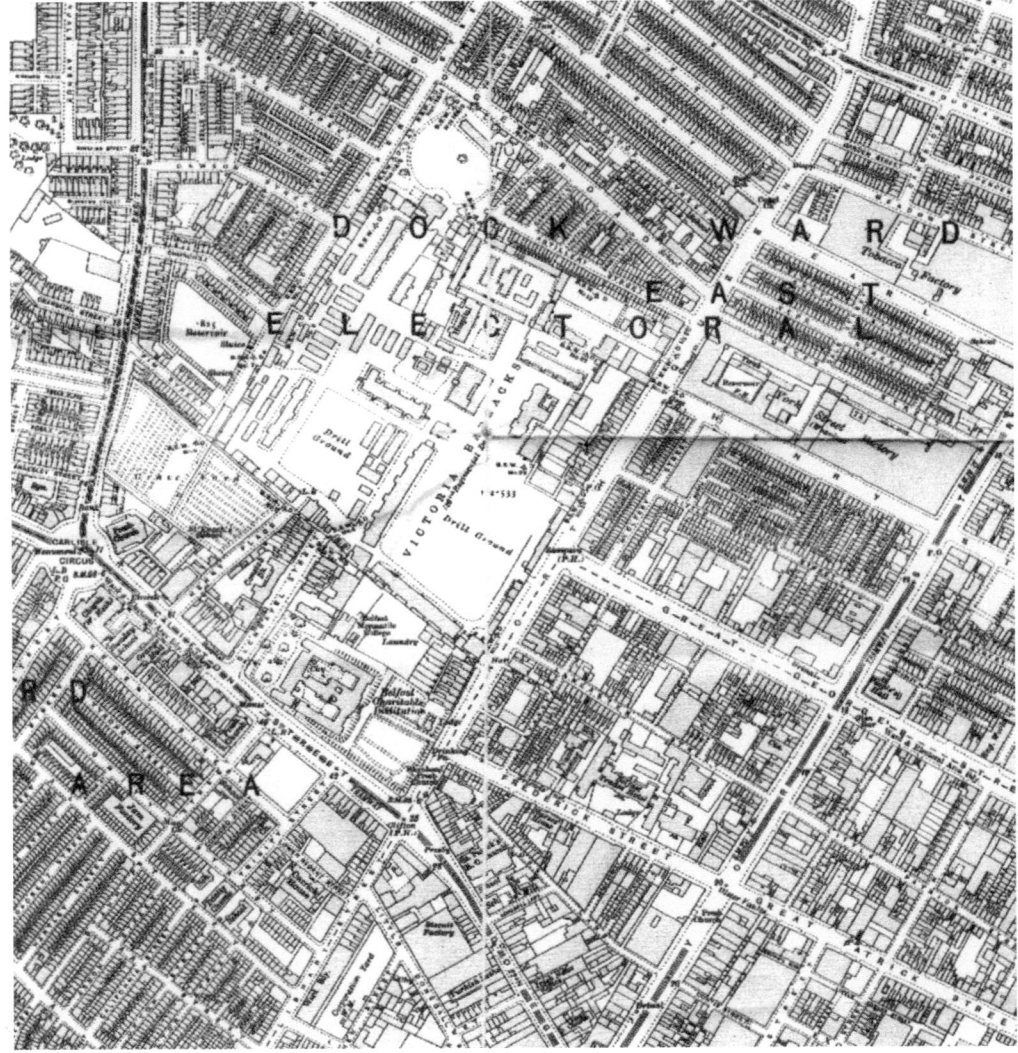

A map showing Victoria Barracks at the time of the tragedy.

Victoria Barracks.

For the next few nights everything was quiet. On the day of the funerals the troops were making preparations for the occasion. When the two bodies were removed from the barrack morgue to the burying ground, all the members of the two companies present at the tragedy were in attendance. When they returned they began to clean their quarters for the following day's officer's inspection. The kit of Private Whelan was removed from his bunk and placed in a storage rack which was in a separate section of their quarters. When the inspection came, the soldiers had been lined up outside in the barrack square, where they had to stand to attention as the officers entered their quarters. When the officers left, the company leader furiously addressed his men concerning the state inside. Back in the quarters all the men's bunks had been disturbed and left untidy and the kit of Private Whelan had been laid out on his bunk, also untidily. The soldiers then believed something 'sinister' was happening and informed their section leader. The section leader believed the men, as he had inspected the quarters before the men had entered the yard. He also knew that no one else was inside the building when the occurrence took place as everyone had been accounted for. A suggestion was made to take turns for someone to stay awake throughout the night to ensure that nothing out of the ordinary took place.

This continued until the next inspection and when nothing else occurred, their duties returned to normal. At this stage, another soldier had taken the bunk of Private Whelan and once again the dead soldier's kit had been stored away. After spending the first night in the bunk the soldier awoke the following morning to find what looked like footprints around his bed.

When the men began to clean their quarters the footprints were washed away, but when the water dried the footprints reappeared. They were washed again and again but there was no change—the footprints always came back. One of the soldiers suggested that the kit of Private Whelan should be placed back on the bunk to see if anything would happen. The kit was taken back and placed on the bunk but the footsteps remained, even after additional cleaning attempts.

The minister of the garrison church was sent for and when he arrived, the soldiers asked him to wash away the footprints. He did so and, like the soldiers, he was shocked to watch the water dry up and the footprints remain. The man who had slept in the bunk was not sleeping there again. He packed up his kit and moved to his original bunk further down the landing and when he did so, the footsteps disappeared. The soldiers then realised what was happening. When the kit of Private Whelan was removed strange incidents began to occur. The troops gathered up Whelan's entire kit and laid it all out on the bunk the way the soldier had done before he died. The incidents stopped.

A few months later the soldiers returned to their home base and another regiment moved in. It is unknown if any of the incidents occurred after this, but there are no records of any. What is known is that strange stories continued in relation to the barracks, stories which continued right up until its demolition. Even then ghostly sightings were reported among the ruins.

'SCOTTIE SHOE' - THE GHOST OF THE GRAND CENTRAL HOTEL

Many of us today still remember the Grand Central Hotel which stood on the site now occupied by the Castle Court shopping centre on Royal Avenue. The hotel itself was a large Victorian building which was built in the year 1885 on a site belonging to the Robb family, owners of a large department store in nearby High Street. The ghost, reputedly one of the gas fitters of this hotel, was said to have haunted it from the date it opened. Nothing much is known about this man other than the fact that he, and later his ghost, was nicknamed 'Scottie Shoe,' which is a strange title, even for a nickname.

Numerous reports about this ghost have been stated but most of them occurred whenever the military first occupied the building. This happened in 1914 when World War One broke out. The military commander for the north received a message from the war office to requisition the Grand Central, and soon after the manager was told to accept no more bookings and to clear the building. This he was compiled to do and after all the staffs were paid off the building was locked up and the keys handed over to the army. A small number of military personnel were placed in charge of the hotel and were ordered to remain within the building to await further instructions. Seventeen soldiers were now staying here and all occupied a row of rooms on the first floor. Each night one of them took a turn to patrol the building and to carry out a fire check, and it was in the execution of this duty that various sightings of this ghost were reported.

On 26 May 1914 it was the turn of William Jenkins, the commanding officer, to do 'the rounds' in the building. A short time later the men were alarmed by the sounds of the officer screaming in the upper floors. They then ran to him, some towards the main stairs and some towards the back stairs which were for the use of staff. He was discovered lying at the foot of the stairs on the landing, very nervous and shaken. The men lifted him and took him back to his quarters where he told them what he had seen.

He stated that he had been walking through the second floor corridor, checking the individual rooms, when he heard a dragging sound coming from the end of the landing. He went to investigate and discovered that the sounds had been coming from a closed section of the building which contained all the gas metres for that landing. Thinking that some of his men were up to something, he slowly turned the handle and rushed in through the door. After doing so he was confronted by the figure of a man making his way towards him, and seconds later he knew that what he was seeing was unusual as the lower part of its legs appeared to be disappearing into the floor. He panicked and ran back towards the stairs but in doing so he dropped his candle and found himself in total darkness. It was then that he started to scream for help.

Still hearing the dragging sound, the officer believed the ghost to still be there so he ran towards the area where the stairs were and, reaching them in darkness, he stumbled down.

Later the incident was discussed at length and the men who ran up the staff stairs were asked if they had seen or heard anything, but none of them had. The men told Jenkins that they believed his story, but this may have been said only because he was their officer. It is also believed that the men ridiculed him behind his back.

A few weeks later the soldiers were removed from the hotel and posted to the front but the commanding officer remained. New recruits were placed in the building and the total number this time was seventy-four, with the whole first floor landing used to house them. Because of his earlier scare, the officer refused to compile the nightly check on the building and ordered one of the new soldiers to do it. The officer told them nothing about the ghostly figure and at nights the men even told each other stories about the hotel which they had made up to scare the others.

A few days after their arrival, two of the men went out together to complete the night patrol. About an hour later the men rushed back to their quarters, out of breath and shaken. They related that they had seen the figure of a man on the second floor corridor and after approaching, discovered that it wasn't a man at all, but in fact appeared to be a ghost. They then ran back towards the stairs and, unlike the officer, they had managed to keep their candles lit. When they got to the quarters and told their stories, the other men thought it was a joke.

Castle Court Shopping Centre, Belfast.

The interior of the Grand Central Hotel.

A few moments later Jenkins came into the room and asked what was going on. Then men told him what had happened and when he heard the story he immediately began to ask questions about what exactly they had seen, asking them to describe it. The other men still took it as a joke but after Jenkins admitted that he had seen the same thing, in the same area, the troops began to believe it. After this the men all refused to carry out this patrol and the building remained unchecked.

A few months later Officer Jenkins and the rest of the soldiers were sent to the trenches where no doubt many of them, if not all, lost their lives. More recruits were sent to the hotel and it was at this stage that the army began to wonder what exactly they were to do with the hotel and why it was seized. The matter was investigated and it turned out that the whole affair was a mistake and that a requisition order, meant for the Grand Central Hotel in Bristol, had been sent to Belfast by mistake. Not wanting to admit to this major embarrassment, the military used the building as the Ministry of Pensions for the troops returning from the front. The military moved out and it was again used as a hotel in 1927.

There were numerous ghost stories told within the hotel but because there are no details of what they were, it can be assumed that they would have been tales to 'break in' new members of staff working in particular sections of the building.

The Grand Central Hotel.

After the outbreak of the present troubles the military again occupied the building from 1971 until 1981. It was used as the city centre headquarters and was also the base for the army bomb squad. Many stories were told of hauntings within the building between soldiers entering in for a new tour of duty but it is not known if any of them were based on the tale of 'Scottie Shoe'? During the 1980s the Grand Central was demolished to clear the site for the construction of the present Castle Court. During this time a story was told about two 'lead liberators' who had got into the site to make off with copper and lead. Apparently one of the pair saw what was believed to be a ghost on the second floor of the building, the same section which 'Scottie Shoe' was said to haunt. Nothing remains of the hotel today but could the same be said about the ghost who occupied it?

The Pipe Lane Mill Haunting

Although not its proper title, the Pipe Lane Mill was a large five-storey building which stood on the site occupied by the present Smithfield Market on Winetavern Street (Pipe Lane was this street's former title). The building was constructed in 1854 by the Smithfield Flax Spinning and Weaving Company and throughout the years, as the demand for linen grew, numerous extensions were added on. The site on which it was built was the ground on which the old Belfast jail stood and the gate lodge of the mill was in fact the residence of the prison's governor.

On Monday 20 January 1902 the workforce reported for duty at the usual time of 6.30 a.m. and after the time permitted for their first break, disaster struck. At approximately 9.30 a.m. an extremely loud crashing sound was heard throughout the mill and moments later it was discovered that a large section of the building had collapsed. Panic immediately broke out as the workers rushed for the nearest exit. Hundreds of tons of masonry and twisted metal had fallen into the courtyard and crushed all the roving sheds below. Those working within them were either killed outright or were seriously injured. As well as the masonry falling many machines fell with it and this included those people who were unfortunate enough to be working at them at that particular time. Soon after, rescue work commenced to uncover the survivors and the bodies of those who were killed. This work continued for a few days until all hope of finding anyone else alive was gone. The following is the list of those who had died:

Ellen Scott, Aged 14, 4 Letitia Street - Doffer.
Alice Cunningham, Aged 20, 17 Jude Street - Reeler.
Mary Burns, Aged 18, 34 California Street - Spinner.
Mary Burke, Aged 19, 39 Arnon Street - Spinner.
Mary Kerr, Aged 20, 9 Union Street - Spinner.
Annie Hunter, Aged 16, 8 Sackville Street - Doffer.
Mrs Davidson, Aged 50, Address Unknown - Reeler.
Mary Williamson, Aged 22, 68 Gulian Street - Spinner.
Ellen Corr, Aged 40, 14 Artillery Street - Preparer.
Alice Mc Donnell, Aged 18, 4 Linton Street - Preparer.
Mary Duff, Aged 60, 23 Wilson Street - Reeler.
Lizzie Campbell, Aged 20, 117 Bristol Street - Reeler.
Martha Mc Auley, Aged 13, 39 Wall Street - Doffer

HAUNTED BELFAST

Pipe Lane Hill.

A large number of people were very seriously injured and at later dates another two victims died in the Royal Hospital, Frederick Street. At the inquests it was found that 'The collapse of the portion of the mill was due to (a) defect at the base of the piers, and are of opinion that the defect could not have been discovered by ordinary inspection, and that no blame can be attached to any person in connection with the accident.' Repair work began on the mill after the inquest was held and within a year the mill was back to its full working capacity.

Soon after tales began to circulate concerning ghostly sightings of some of the people killed. One of these was the sighting by a number of mill girls of an elderly woman who appeared at one of the machines which stood on the repaired section of the floor. The woman stood for around thirty seconds and then moved to go around the machine. One of the women who saw her immediately stated that she had an uncanny likeness to Mary Duff, who had been killed, and when she went over to the machine to investigate the woman had completely disappeared. It was impossible for her to have gone anywhere without being seen by any of the other women and, because they were on the fourth floor, there was no where else she could have gone. This strange sighting went on for a number of years and even one of the senior staff claimed to have seen her. On that occasion one of the safety inspectors had been doing routine checks when he saw an old woman at one of the machines (it had been in the evening and all the mill girls had gone home a few hours previously). He went over to see what she was doing and as he did so, he lost sight of her and the woman had disappeared. Knowing that something odd was occurring he immediately reported the incident to the watchman who informed him of the story and confided that a number of the girls had also seen the old woman. He then went back to the factory and completed his check without further incident. The following day he went to the workrooms and began to ask questions about the old woman. Some of the workers who claimed to have seen her told him about their experiences and described the woman. All the tales, including those of the safety officers', matched.

Another sighting was that of another woman who, it was claimed, was seen on a number of occasions going down the spiral staircase of the mill. The first time this occurred was when one of the workers was coming up the stairs and saw another woman coming down. The pair passed each other and, because the woman was unknown to her, the girl looked behind her, but the woman had disappeared. Knowing that this was impossible in the seconds that had passed since she had turned, she rushed down after her but there was no sight of her whatsoever. When she came back up she said nothing about the matter – that is until another sighting occurred a few months later.

On this occasion one of the girls came into the workroom and stated that she was rushing up the stairs and that someone was coming down. She said that when they met the other had vanished in front of her and that she had paused for a few seconds before she realised what had happened. A few of the others went out to investigate and again there was no sign of the person she had seen. It was then that the first sighting was reported.

Both the old woman and the girl on the stairs were claimed to have been seen on a number of occasions after this, and it soon after they became known as the 'Pipe Lane Mill Hauntings.'

A few years later the mill had shut down and in 1930 the property was sold to the London Midland & Scottish Railway Co. Most of the mill was demolished and the weaving shop was converted into a bus station. It was used for this purpose until the 1970s and no further sightings were reported.

A Tragic Belfast Haunting

Belfast, like all cities and towns throughout Ireland, has many diverse ghost stories to tell. Most of these stories are usually contained within the residential communities. One area which is lacking in these stories is the commercial centre. One reason for this may be due to the fact that very few people actually live in this area and any supernatural occurrences could possibly go unnoticed. This was not always the case. In Victorian Belfast almost every hotel and guesthouse was said to have been haunted, including those in the city centre. At this time a lot of people actually lived in the city centre and tales of the supernatural were in abundance. Even the large department stores were said to contain ghosts, with one of the most famous being that which was said to haunt Robb's Department Store. There were many different stories told in relation to this and the one thing which they all seem to have in common was that all told of objects being thrown around. This sort of supernatural behaviour is known as the 'poltergeist' and although they are better known for throwing objects there are a number of incidents where they simply moved them.

One such place in Belfast's city centre where this was said to have occurred was in the old Corporation Gas Office which was situated in Queen Street. During the early decades of the last century there were a number of regular occurrences which took place and which no one was ever able to fully explain. On many occasions when staff opened up, it was discovered that various heavy items of furniture had been moved around. Although these were generally tables and chairs, there were a number of occasions when almost everything had been moved. All reasonable explanations were ruled out for a number of different reasons. When these occurrences did take place it was at night when the building was unoccupied. Anyone who would have wanted to move the furniture would have to break in and there was never any sign of forced entry. Anyone with keys who would wish to do it would have to bring a number of people with them to move the heavier objects which were sometimes shifted. Another reason for dismissing this explanation was the fact that these strange occurrences were taking place over a thirty year period. If anyone had been responsible then there is no doubt that they would have been discovered over such a time span. Nothing was ever seen or heard and no other types of activity were ever reported. The staff seemed to be in no danger and appeared to be victims of the mischievous supernatural phenomena - the poltergeist.

But why was it occurring in a non-residential building in the heart of Belfast? Poltergeist activity is generally centred on people, in particular young children, and lasts for a short period of time. This was different. As stated, no one lived in the building and nothing ever occurred when the building was occupied during office hours. There were those who believed that the activity was centred around someone who had died as a result of gas poisoning, but if this was the case then there would be no doubt that it would be difficult to pin it down, as an average of 130 people per year were killed in gas accidents, although there are a number of supernatural cases relating to some of these tragedies.

One of these centred on the deaths of two sisters in a house in North Belfast. Number 100 Crumlin Road was a large terrace house which stood near to where the present courthouse stands. In the early years of the last century, a family named Spence bought the house which had been lying derelict for over forty years. As could be expected a lot of cleaning had to be completed and a lot of old furniture dumped, but the family decided to keep an old piano which stood in the front parlour. The Spence's settled into their new home and after a short period a number of strange occurrences took place. The first was when the family noticed a very strong smell of gas which disappeared after they turned it off at the mains and opened all the windows. They then called in the corporation gas department who double-checked everything and found it to be functional. At this stage Mr Spence thought that one of the gas lanterns or the cooker had been left on and dismissed the whole subject as an accident. Afterwards he began to take more care and ensured that all gas appliances were switched off before he retired each evening.

A few weeks later the same thing occurred again, only this time he moved his family from the house and went immediately to the nearby Landscape Terrace Police Barracks where he reported the matter. The police contacted the gas department who sent out two workmen to see to the problem. When the men arrived they opened all the windows to allow the gas out and set about finding the fault. As in the first case, no fault was found and the workmen went into the house next door to check their gas outlets, but again everything was in order. The following day the gas department began work to replace all the gas pipes in the both houses and this was complete within a few days.

A number of weeks later the family were awakened by the sound of the piano playing downstairs and, again, a strong smell of gas. Mr Spence ventured downstairs and was closely followed by his family, but when he reached the parlour door the playing suddenly stopped. He went into the parlour and found that everything was in order and that the piano flap was closed. At the same time he and his family noticed that the smell of gas had also disappeared. The following day they had the piano checked to see if it had any type of novelty device built in, but they were informed that it was just a normally functioning piano. Mystified, the family put the blame on a rodent such as a rat or mouse but could never offer any explanation as to why it was playing in tune or where the smell of gas came from. For the next seven months all was quiet within the house and none of the past strange occurrences were taking place - that is until 12 March 1919. This time the family were once again wakened by the piano playing and, like the first time, the smell of gas was again present. Two of the youngest children came rushing downstairs screaming that someone had been coughing in their upstairs bedroom. Mr Spence investigated and found the children's bedroom empty. He then went downstairs in the darkness (he could not light any candles because of the gas) and when he reached the bottom the piano ceased and the fumes disappeared. For the rest of the evening the family stayed together in the backroom with the children sleeping in the chairs. The following day Mr Spence realised that there must have been a supernatural phenomenon surrounding the piano and immediately arranged for it to be dumped. After this, all the strange occurrences stopped.

Like every other story centred on any supernatural theme, it is generally believed that there must be some sort of explanation and that any connections with past events are pure coincidence. However, the events which occurred in this house and their connection with a past event are more than pure coincidence.

HAUNTED BELFAST

In June 1878 two elderly sisters named Jane and Mary McClement, aged eighty-two and seventy-seven, died in this house. Their house was being decorated which meant they had to sleep in one of the attic bedrooms. At their inquest it was revealed that one of the workmen failed to re-connect a gas light fitting and the two sisters died in their beds of suffocation. They were discovered the following day by a Constable O'Brien who had been called in by a servant girl. The house had lain empty for over forty years due to a legal problem on ownership, and Mr Spence was the first to live in it after the two unfortunate sisters.

The connection with the gas is obvious and Miss Mary McClement, it was discovered, was a fond pianist. By far the most interesting connection is the fact that the sisters died in the same room from which the two children heard the coughing sounds.

Another similar incident in which gas fumes were detected occurred some time later in 1935 in the south of the city. A family living in a house in Linfield Street were constantly disturbed at gas fumes stinking out their house and, like the previous incidents, nothing was ever discovered when the pipes were checked. The family were adamant that there was a gas leak and when their neighbours were called into the house they also noticed the fumes. Gas officials checked every pipe, connection and appliance but everything was fine. After a period of around six weeks, the fumes disappeared as suddenly as they began.

Sometime later one of the family were talking with some of the neighbours when they were told that a tragedy had occurred in this house some years previously. This occurred a few days before Christmas in 1913 when an entire family were asphyxiated, one fatally. William Galbraith and his family were in bed when gas fumes began to fill the house. The following morning when the family arose everyone was extremely weak and Mr Galbraith had been frothing at the mouth. Medical assistance was sought but before the doctor arrived, Mr Galbraith had died.

Corporation gas officials later arrived and, after carrying out an extensive inspection of the supply, no defect was found in any of the pipes, however the strong smell of gas was still present. Additional checks were then carried out on the gas pipes in the immediate area and a leak was discovered at the rear of a shop in Sandy Row which backed on to the house. The gas officials then stated that gas coming from this leak made its way through the earth and then seeped up through the floor of the Galbraith house. This was an extremely rare occurrence and was only discovered after a full investigation. What was never discovered was the source of the gas fumes in the same house which aggravated a family for six weeks in 1935.

Almost a year after the tragic death in Linfield Street, another incident occurred in the Carrick Hill area which also involved gas and which led to an extremely violent paranormal occurrence. On 6 November 1914, Edward McGrath burgled a house at No 11 Upton Street. Once there, he dismantled the gas meter and stole nine pence. He then hurried out of the house and left the disconnected meter lying on the floor with gas pumping out of the pipes. At the same time two girls, Edith Bruce and Madge Briggs, were upstairs, too terrified to come down to investigate the sounds. After a while, both began to slowly come downstairs. Edith Bruce was at the front as she was holding a lighted candle. Once they reached the hallway, she slowly opened the door to the room where they had heard the sounds.

Constable Fox of the R.I.C. was on duty on the Old Lodge Road when he heard a massive explosion. He rushed to Upton Street and where he observed that all the windows of no. 11 had been blown out and that some of the neighbours were approaching the house. Screaming was heard coming from the house and when the constable rushed in he saw two girls in the hallway, in flames. He took off his greatcoat and used it to drag one of the girls out into the street where the flames were extinguished by the neighbours. He again used his coat to get the other girl out. A number of solders who had been passing along Carrick Hill on their way to Victoria Barracks came on the scene and carried both girls to the medical hall of Dr Thompson in nearby Peter's Hill. From here they were then conveyed to the Mater Infirmorum Hospital where they both lay in a critical condition. Two days later twenty-two year old Edith Bruce died. A full police investigation was then carried out and Edward McGrath was arrested and later convicted.

At the same time as the girl's death, loud screams were heard coming from no. 11. They seemed to be coming from the back of the house and continued as a crowd began to gather outside. A number of men began to remove hording which had been placed to secure the house. When a small gap was created three of them entered. The screaming stopped immediately and when one of them reached the foot of the stairs he was violently thrown back down the hallway and into the two men behind him. These two rushed back out of the house and out into the safety of the street, leaving the other to fend for himself. Some of the other men then rushed to get him and when one of them looked through he saw the man lying injured on the floor. He squeezed through and helped out the injured man. There was never a recurrence of this behaviour, or of the screams of what was undoubtedly a supernatural occurrence which lasted less than five minutes, and which one man had the marks to prove.

The Gas Office.

Another gas tragedy which led to reports of paranormal behaviour again occurred shortly before Christmas in 1939, this time in Caledon Street in the Shankill area. At this time the Second World War was still in its infancy and many men from the area were joining the ranks of the British Army, one of them being Robert Porter. Mr Porter went to serve as a dispatch rider in England, leaving his wife and five children behind. Mrs Porter was looking after four of her children in their Caledon Street home while the other, thirteen year old Margaret, was still in hospital recovering from burns which she received the previous Christmas after spilling a pot of scalding water over herself. Everything was fine until Wednesday 14 December when disaster struck.

In the late afternoon the neighbours became concerned when they had not seen Mrs Porter all day. None of her children had been at school and were not playing in the street. Mrs Fox, who lived two doors from the Porter's house, went to the house with a Mrs Mehaffy and Mrs Milligan where they noticed that the blinds were still closed. 'We agreed to open the door and see if Mrs Porter was still in the house,' stated Mrs Fox to the police, 'Mrs Porter was a wee bit odd and would not like us to do anything like that, but we agreed to apologise to her if we found her all right.'

Crumlin Road House.

The front door was found to be locked and the keyhole stuffed with paper, said Mrs Fox, who added that when the three women got into the hall, after forcing the door, they discovered that the inner glass door was also locked. 'When we got the glass door open we smelled gas and had fears that something serious had happened. There was no one in the small room behind. Mrs Mehaffy was going upstairs, but she turned and came down again. We then sent for the police.'

Constables Shannon and Moore arrived and when they entered the upstairs bedroom they discovered that it was full of gas. Norah Porter and her children Robert (7), Leslie (5), Norah (3), and Thomas (seven months) were all lying on the bed, dead.

The tragedy had all the signs of suicide/murder, but at the inquest the blame was attached to an unnamed workman who had been fixing one of the lanterns in the bedroom. Unable to do so, this workman decided that a new lantern was needed and until he obtained it he blocked the open end of the pipe with a cork. Because the pressure of gas is heavier at night, it is believed that the cork was pushed out and the room filled with gas. The City Coroner, Dr H Lowe, launched a verbal attack on this unknown workman before returning a verdict of accidental death.

It was shortly after this tragic occurrence that strange behaviour began to be noticed around this house. Those who lived in the house facing it claimed that they had seen the curtains move and that the figure of a woman matching Mrs Porter's description was seen behind them. After this occurred a few times, some of the neighbours decided to enter the house and see if there was anyone there, but there never was. On another occasion when the same figure was seen the house was entered from the front and the back and again no one was discovered. People from all around the district began to assemble around the house to see if they could witness this strange occurrence, but it is presently unknown if anything was ever seen by them. This strange figure was seen on a number of additional occasions and was reported to have disappeared whenever Mr Porter returned.

These are just a few of the paranormal incidents which occurred in Belfast and which were connected to tragedies involving gas. As previously stated it would be impossible to conclude if any of them were in any way responsible for the occurrences which took place in the old gas office, or if they were as a result of any other gas tragedy.

Today the old gas office is long gone and was replaced with a modern building. Nothing unusual was ever reported in this building which closed down when the gas supply to Belfast was discontinued. Today it is a craft store.

Ghostly nun at Ballynafeigh

A considerable number of ghost stories involve buildings and people in the local religious communities; stories that recount hauntings around rectories, priories and many that involve nuns and priests, such as the nun that is said to haunt the Bank Underground Station in London. Workmen who were building Bank Station in the 1800s roused the spirit of the so-called 'Black Nun'. The nun's brother, Philip Whitehead, was a cashier and was executed in 1811 for forgery. The nun, Sarah, wearing black, waited for him outside the bank every evening for forty years until she died. To this day, it is said that she still searches for him along the platforms.

Another famous ghost story concerning a nun is that of Borley Rectory. This ghost was seen so often at Essex's Borley Rectory that the house was said to be the most haunted in England.

On one bone-chilling occasion the first hint that the ghost was near was when the diners seated at the table felt a sudden chill in the room. A hush fell over the group. 'Look', one of the diners whispered to the others, 'there she is'.

Everyone turned and clearly saw the woman's ashen face, framed by the grey hood of her habit, peering at them through the window. Cold chills ran up their spines. This was the nun of Borley Rectory - the same woman who had died a horrible death on that spot centuries before.

Although she has been seen throughout the house and grounds of Borley Rectory, the dining room window seemed to be a special place that belonged to her and her alone. The ghostly nun was seen there hundreds of times, by hundreds of witnesses. Her appearances were so frequent, and so unnerving, that the window was finally bricked up.

The infamous Borley Rectory was destroyed by a fire of mysterious origin in 1939. Even after the fire, strange events continued to occur in the ashes. In 1944, *Life* magazine photographer David E. Scherman, *Time-Life* archivist Cynthia Ledsham and writer Noel F. Busch were visiting the ruins with paranormal investigator Harry Price. About four feet above the ground, the group spotted a heavy brick rising in mid-air without benefit of human hands. In spite of his excitement, Scherman was able to hold his camera steady enough to snap a clear picture.

Borley Rectory was built in 1863 by the Rev. Henry Bull in Essex, across the road from the ancient Borley Church where he preached. (A church building of some kind had stood on the spot since the 12th century.) The new rectory was a Gothic mix of brick and stone and, in popular imagination, looked exactly like a haunted house ought to look.

Over the years, numerous unexplained incidents occurred in the house and the building became so infamous that in 1928 the current occupant of the rectory, Rev. Guy Eric Smith, contacted the London *Daily Mirror* asking for help. The *Mirror* sent a reporter, C.V. Wall, who patiently listened to the tales told by the Smiths describing poltergeist activity in the house. The Smiths described moans, hearing footsteps, dodging small pebbles hurled by unknown assailants and, of course, of seeing the ever-present apparition of the nun. When the report was published in the paper, two things happened. The first was that gawkers arrived in droves with their incessant demands to see the inside of the rectory, which worried the Smiths nearly to death. The second thing that happened was that famed ghost hunter Harry Price came to call.

Price spent the next ten years investigating the house and wrote two books on the subject. When the Smiths were forced to move out of the house because of the flood of unwanted publicity, the Rev. Lionel Foyster and his wife Marianne moved in. For some reason the presence of Marianne caused the ghostly activity to increase. The nun even attempted to contact Marianne by scrawling pleas to her on the walls. Much of the writing looked like the scribbling of a child, but sometimes the message was clear: 'Marianne ... please help get ...' said one. Marianne wrote beneath it in reply, 'I cannot understand. Tell me more.' Unintelligible gibberish was written beneath that.

Price had a theory as to why the nun haunted the house and recounted an old legend to back up his argument. Before Henry VIII of England broke with Rome in 1534 and established the Anglican Church, England was a Catholic nation. A priory once stood on the exact spot where Borley would be built. According to the church, both nuns and priests were to remain celibate under pain of excommunication, or worse. But love did blossom.

A novice (a nun who had not taken her final vows) of the Nunnery of Burnes seven miles away, fell in love with a young monk of Borley. Their meetings, by necessity, were clandestine, lest their superiors discover their sacrilege.

But suspicions were aroused in both camps and word leaked back to the authorities. Traps were laid and the lovers were discovered. The terrified couple tried to get away. Unfortunately, they were not fast enough and both were captured trying to flee in a carriage driven by a friend.

The young monk was put to death along with the coachman. The nun suffered an even more horrible fate. She was walled up alive, to serve penitence and to die, in the vaults below the priory. It was her ghost, as well as the monk's, that walked Borley Rectory.

Between 1930 and 1935, Price said that he recorded at least 2,000 paranormal events in the house, including pebble-throwing, cold spots, wall writing, objects being moved and the mysterious appearances of an ancient Catholic medallion. Critics accused Foyster and Price of conspiring to make Borley Rectory a kind of Amityville. In fact, much of Price's investigations were later discredited and he was branded a charlatan. While Price was alive (he died in 1948) he swore that his research was authentic and that he would haunt Borley himself to get the facts and then share them with the world from beyond the grave. (It was reported that he did just that, through a psychic).

Captain W. H. Gregson bought Borley Rectory in 1937, knowing full well its haunted reputation. He enlisted Price to investigate the house further. Gregson even wrote a few articles about the place himself. Then, one night in 1939, Borley Rectory was consumed by fire. By the time the flames had run their course, only the study brick walls remained.

The fire itself remains a mystery. Alan William Gregson claims that his father was shelving books in the library when an oil lamp accidentally tipped over. Another son, Anthony, had a different explanation for the fire. In a letter to Richard Lee-Van den Daele he wrote 'My father, Capt. W.H. Gregson, bought Borley Rectory as a real estate venture around 1937, at which time it was classified by a prominent spiritualist, Harry Price, as the most haunted house in England.' When this didn't pan out he torched it for insurance.

The Borley Rectory.

In any event, the ghostly nun of Borley Rectory was said to have migrated to Borley Church across the road after the fire. But her powers to appear to the living are apparently on the wane. Nowadays she is only seen occasionally.

The single pattern relating to the ghosts connected with nuns is their tragic nature and the Belfast story is no different. It was centred on the old Convent of the Good Shepherd at Ballynafeigh and, while actual sightings were rare, the noises certainly were not. At the turn of the last century and the latter years of the 1800s terrifying screams would often be heard throughout the convent and always during the day. Young girls based here would be quite scared but seasoned nuns would often just tut and state 'there goes Ellen again.'

On rare occasions the ghost of a young teenage girl would be seen and completely disappear in just a few seconds. This went on for around twenty years and seemed to cease just before the outbreak of the First World War. But who was Ellen?

Ellen was an orphan who had decided to join the nuns who had raised her. Not long after her seventeenth birthday in March 1879 she had been working in the washhouse lifting buckets of boiling water out of a large boiler. While doing so she had lost her balance and fell head first into the boiler which contained a large quantity of boiling water. Hearing her screams, the others in the washroom rushed to the boiler and, using poles, lifted her out, but she had been scalded in a frightful manner. A doctor was sent for and every effort was made to alleviate the poor girl's suffering but it was obvious that she was going to die. Later that night she did so, after a tremendous amount of suffering.

Like all ghost stories there is a lot of mystery attached to them and one mystery relating to this story is why did the strange occurrences not begin until some years later, and why did they cease as suddenly as they began?